Lifestorming

Lifestorming

CREATING MEANING
AND ACHIEVEMENT
IN YOUR CAREER AND LIFE

Alan Weiss │ Marshall Goldsmith

WILEY

Cover Design: Paul McCarthy
Cover Art: Getty images © Mimi Haddon

Published by John Wiley & Sons, Inc., Hoboken, New Jersey.
Published simultaneously in Canada.

For general information about our other products and services, please contact our Customer Care
Department within the United States at (800) 762-2974, outside the United States at (317) 572-3993
or fax (317) 572-4002.

Wiley publishes in a variety of print and electronic formats and by print-on-demand. Some material
included with standard print versions of this book may not be included in e-books or in
print-on-demand. If this book refers to media such as a CD or DVD that is not included in the version
you purchased, you may download this material at http://booksupport.wiley.com. For more
information about Wiley products, visit www.wiley.com.

Library of Congress Cataloging-in-Publication Data

Names: Weiss, Alan, 1946– author. | Goldsmith, Marshall, author.
Title: Lifestorming : creating meaning and achievement in your career and
    life / Alan Weiss, Marshall Goldsmith.
Description: Hoboken : Wiley, 2017. | Includes index. | Description based on
    print version record and CIP data provided by publisher; resource not viewed.
Identifiers: LCCN 2017010479 (print) | ISBN 9781119366126 (hardback)
Subjects: LCSH: Self-actualization (Psychology) | Motivation (Psychology) |
    Decision making. | Problem solving. | BISAC: BUSINESS & ECONOMICS /
    Motivational. | BUSINESS & ECONOMICS / Decision-Making & Problem Solving.
Classification: LCC BF637.S4 (ebook) | LCC BF637.S4 W4445 2017 (print) | DDC
    650.1–dc23
LC record available at https://lccn.loc.gov/2017010479

ISBN: 978-1-119-36612-6 (hhk)
ISBN: 978-1-119-36629-4 (ebk)
ISBN: 978-1-119-36628-7 (ebk)

Printed in the United States of America

10 9 8 7 6 5 4 3 2 1

Contents

Introduction

In our culture, we are bombarded by messages that essentially say, "Change! Improve! Get better!" We're surrounded day and night by these directives, whether they come from the diet industry, the vast trove of self-improvement literature, or the rhetoric of politicians . . . even toothpaste ads are aspirational!

Given how overwhelming these messages are, it's tempting to simply shut them out. Who can possibly follow all that advice? But we still give it half an ear because we know, deep down, that we *could* change for the better, if only we knew how. But that's the bedeviling question: How? Most of us try to change for years, without that change ever becoming permanent. We are left wondering how we can become the people we want to be—the people we know we can be.

The great Western disease is "I will be happy when!" When I get the money, the status, the position, the BMW, that special person. The great Western art form is something that sounds like this: "There were many people. The people were all sad. They decided to spend money. They bought a product. Then they all became happy!"

This message is called a commercial. How many of these have you seen? How many times have you been barraged by this same message? It is no wonder that we tend to look for the quick fix and the easy answer. We have been programmed, over and over again, to think this way.

Advertising presents an easy solution: Buy the product! But as anyone who has tried this strategy knows, real change is never that easy. While change is not easy, it is possible, and that's what *Lifestorming* offers. In this book, we'll guide you as you think about your goals— why you chose them, how you can achieve them, and (critically) how they can evolve over time to reflect your changing priorities.

The great fallacy of creating lasting change is that we only need to do it once. As the Greek philosopher Heraclitus said, we never step twice into the same river. As soon as we're done achieving one benchmark, another appears before us. That's especially true in these volatile, unpredictable times, when business, technology, and just about everything else is changing at unprecedented speeds.

In this environment, character and an underlying sense of self-worth are more important than ever. Without them, it's too easy to drift away from what's really most important. In this book, authored by two of the most highly regarded executive and entrepreneurial coaches, you'll gain insight into why so many of us end up in places we never meant to go. Consider this a map for getting on the right track.

Before getting started, a little bit about us:

Alan Weiss: I'm an expert in human performance and growth. I began my career working globally for 15 years with Fortune 500 firms, before transitioning to working with entrepreneurs and owners of boutique firms. I've written 50 books, which appear in 12 languages and dozens of editions, including the 25-year bestseller *Million Dollar Consulting*. I'm the only nonjournalist in history to have received the Lifetime Achievement Award from the American Press Institute. I live in East Greenwich, Rhode Island, with my wife of 48 years, Maria, and we have two children and two grandchildren—with more expected! I'm a member of the National Speakers Association Hall of Fame® and a Fellow of the Institute of Management Consultants.

Marshall Goldsmith: As an executive coach and business educator, my mission is to help successful leaders achieve positive, lasting change in behavior, for themselves, their people, and their teams. In addition to advising more than 120 major CEOs and their management teams, I'm the author or editor of 35 books, which have sold over 2 million copies, been translated into 32 languages, and become bestsellers in 12 countries. I constantly crisscross the globe to speak, teach, and coach. On one airline alone, I have more than 11 million frequent flyer miles! I'm married to the wonderful Lyda, and we also have two children and two grandchildren.

This book is written from Alan's perspective (the "I" you'll be reading about is Alan—unless otherwise noted). Marshall's point of view comes through in the approaches outlined and through some of his personal anecdotes. We have different, yet complementary, backgrounds. I (Alan) am a world authority in providing business advice to entrepreneurial leaders and individual consultants. My (Marshall's) expertise is providing behavioral coaching to leaders in extremely large organizations. While we both work with very successful people, we also work with different types of people. This book is intended to combine our knowledge in a way that can help almost anyone who has a sincere desire to achieve positive, lasting change in behavior.

No two coaches—and no two people—agree on everything, and we're no exception! But we share a fundamental belief in the power of you, the reader, to change. We know it won't be easy. We've seen powerful and influential leaders struggle with this stuff, time and again. But we also know it's eminently possible. So let's get started!

1 | Setting Our Own Aspirations

How We Can Become Programmed

Our natural human tendency is to think of ourselves as independent and authentic—authors of our own destinies. But that's a tall order and much tougher than it seems. Bombarded by external triggers and expectations, we can easily fall into roles and patterns established for us by other people.

Why can it be so hard to resist when someone assigns us a role and expects us to live out this role? I find it fascinating to watch this play out among professional role-players—actors. Some actors are true chameleons, morphing from one part to the next. Others seem to believe they are who they depict, developing attitudes and behaviors consistent with the characters they've played. Marlon Brando was famous for staying in role even when the cameras weren't on. William Shatner often seemed to be Captain James Kirk from *Star Trek*— even when not on the *Starship Enterprise*. Remember the famous ads, still parodied today—"I'm not a doctor, though I play one on television"—in which the actor proceeded—attired in white medical coat—to dispense health information? He was convincing because he began to believe in his own authority.

We often unconsciously become programmed to believe we are someone and then proceed to live our lives trying to fill that role. However, it's often the wrong role: not right for us, and sometimes even harmful.

For years people told me I should become a lawyer. In grammar school and high school I was told I argued well and debated effectively. At Rutgers, I majored in political science, a natural precursor to law school. I did well enough on the LSAT (Law School Admission Test) to earn a full scholarship to Rutgers Law.

There was only one problem. Over that summer, I realized I didn't want to be a lawyer. I never had dreams of working in criminal defense, or as a prosecutor, or settling estates, or refereeing divorces, or working for an organization's legal department. These are great aspirations— but they just weren't mine. I had different dreams, which initially didn't please those who wanted a legal career for me. My parents, who never had money, viewed law as a distinguished and high-earning profession. My teachers wanted it for me too. When I visited the dean of admissions to tell her to give the scholarship to someone else, she actually reached across the desk to try to grab my wrist! Thankfully, I didn't give into that pressure, and today I have a career I love.

A great many people follow their parents into a profession, even when they don't feel any passion for it themselves. A friend of mine followed his father into dentistry, believing it was a good way to make money in the medical field without becoming a physician. Although being a dentist is a great career for many professionals, it was not for him. Too late, he realized he essentially disliked pushing a high-speed drill an eighth of an inch from patients' tongues day in and day out. But by then his practice was paying for private school tuitions, his own educational debt, and all the trappings of an upper middle-class life. Trying another career at his age would have come at a tremendous cost. This conundrum isn't unique to dentistry, of course. Numerous professions represent a well-trodden path that is easier to follow than to leave.

This pattern can be also be influenced by siblings. Brothers and sisters are highly influenced by their sibs, and tend to play the same sports, or become cheerleaders, or join the band (and play the same instrument)—or do just the opposite to escape the comparisons. These are roles that have been established as successful, drawing praise from others, and creating a precedent to follow or from which to flee.

Thus, unseen by the naked eye, we, without thinking about it, may do our best to become the person we were programmed to be rather than the person who, in our hearts, we want to be!

Case Study

I was coaching the former vice chair of a large financial institution. He loved helping people and wanted to be a consultant after his mandatory retirement. His face lit up when he discussed the possibility of being an advisor to other executives.

Surprisingly, he seemed very curious when I asked him if he would be interested if another vice chair position became available. He asked me if I knew about such a position, how much it paid, and the size of the organization.

When I reminded him of his previous discussion about being a consultant, he immediately changed course, thanked me, and mentioned that he had become so used to focusing on money and status that he had temporarily forgotten that he was already rich and wanted to spend the rest of this life doing what *he* most valued.

Some very prestigious jobs are actually a poor fit when you consider the applicant's true aspirations. Retiring executives or admirals might be flattered by offers of a college presidency, for example, something others might ooh and ah at. They may have a vision of a job that allows them to serve as the public face of a venerable institution, leading great discourse and inspiring younger generations. The actual work of a college president, however, may involve sparring with tenured faculty, negotiating the demands of students, and meeting stringent fund-raising goals. Anyone who takes a job like that just because of the title and honorifics is likely to feel disappointed and betrayed. If a different person took the same job with a clear goal of improving higher education, though, she might find the role incredibly fulfilling.

An Evolutionary Journey

We're talking about taking an *evolutionary journey* through life. A journey without a "there." Gertrude Stein coined the epithet "There is no *there*, there" when speaking of Oakland, California. But we mean exactly that. Your "there" is constantly migrating (we'll discuss metamorphosis and change in Chapter 3).

The evolving you is not a moving target, but pursues a moving target.

Milepost

Be careful that your "there" is not created by someone else or some external force, such as Facebook. Your "there" can, and often should, be constantly moving as your experiences, successes, and perspective change. Our bar may well become higher and higher as we journey through life.

An initial question becomes: To what extent is your journey one of internal control, and to what extent one of external control? Do social and normative pressures have a legitimate role in who you are to become? Figure 1.1 illustrates these relationships.

We're using the following definitions:

Control: The power to influence or direct.
Internal: The power that is believed by the performers to be theirs; within their purview.

External: The power that is believed by the performers to be wielded by others or by random events.

When we believe that both internal and external control are low (lower left), we're merely taking a random walk. (A more graphic manner to describe this quadrant is *chaos*: complete disorder and confusion.) I'm reminded of the classic story of the drunk accosted by the bartender and told to get out, who replies, "I didn't walk in here and I'm not leaving."

Many people arise each day simply awaiting what occurs, without the intention of exerting themselves on the world. We see this in circumstances where external direction has been removed advertently or inadvertently (the leader of a group suddenly dies, or is delayed in arriving, or is having a bad day) and no one chooses to step forward into the vacuum. People mill about or drift away. Nothing productive occurs. This is much rarer among entrepreneurs, who realize (and are gratified) that they must make their own plans work, must achieve their own aspirations.

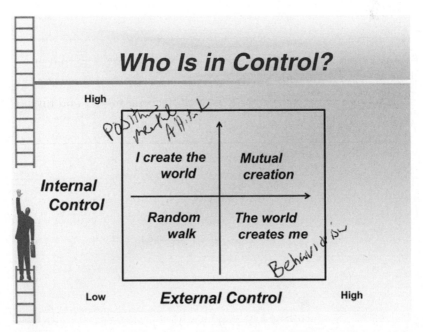

Figure 1.1   Relationship of Internal and External Control

When internal control is seen as high and external control as low (upper left) there is the belief that "I create the world." When carried to an extreme this can lead to narcissism and imperiousness, as well as to a false belief in one's abilities (and to being seen by others as the proverbial empty suit, or in Texas as "big hat, no cattle").

Another version of this belief is illustrated by the classic motivational speech in which the speaker exhorts the audience to overcome fears simply by telling themselves they can or by emulating some deeply dramatic challenge that the speaker has overcome and wrestled to the ground.

One of the funniest examples of the weakness of belief in solely internal control is Bob Newhart's classic routine of a psychologist who charges only a dollar a minute for a maximum of five minutes because his consistent advice to any dysfunctional habit or irrational belief is: "Just stop it!"[1]   *Stop it*

Case Study

I was once president of a company owned by a wealthy insurance magnate and financier. This man believed strongly in a positive mental attitude. He preached this philosophy as the route to success and the cause of his own fortune of over $450 million.

I wondered if he had his etiology (cause and effect) mixed up: that he had a positive mental attitude *because* he had earned $450 million in the insurance business, not vice versa. At one point I joked that if he wanted everyone to have a positive mental attitude he should give them all $450 million.

I was fired not long after—which taught me that even if a positive mental attitude does not guarantee millions in riches, it does tend to help you keep your job.

---

[1] Bob Newhart, "Stop It," YouTube video, OneTrueMedia.com, uploaded by Josh Huynh September 1, 2010, www.youtube.com/watch?v=Ow0lr63y4Mw.

Today, there is a major industry dedicated to convincing people that control of their lives is totally personal and achievable. The highly paid speakers in this industry may be thriving more than their customers. If we truly had total control over our lives, none of us would choose to get sick or eventually die.

We are great believers in positive mental attitude. We believe that helping people to become more motivated about taking control of their own lives is a noble goal. We also believe that the reality of what we can control needs to be balanced with the acknowledgment of what we cannot control.

In the bottom right of Figure 1.1 we have high external control and low internal control. In other words, the world creates and directs us, a Calvinistic sort of predestination. In more modern times this condition has been represented by B. F. Skinner, the psychologist and behaviorist who believed that human behavior could be controlled and predicted. He advocated programmed learning and similar educational practices to train people to whatever ends were desired. Skinner believed that external stimulus was more powerful than individuals' internal control.

We believe Skinner's work sheds some very valuable light on human behavior, but it falls far short of explaining all of it. While our environments are powerful, so are we. I recall hearing many years ago, but can't recall who said, "We train animals, but educate people." You can teach people to perform repetitive tasks—a feature of the training industry that sprang up in response to the world wars—but you can't train people to be enthusiastic, or motivated, or have high energy. That comes from within.

If your belief is that others not only can determine but are responsible for what you become, then you are in a position of surrender. This is the professional victim, who constantly blames the system, or "them," and feels no power. Victims have no inclination to create their own change initiatives. One of the greatest expenses for any company is absenteeism and the greatest cause of absenteeism is stress, and stress is often caused by the feeling that one has no inkling of what may happen tomorrow and no influence over it.

Corey Circle of Control

and Influence

In the extreme case this belief is that the journey has already been mapped and the roads already paved.

This now takes us to the upper right quadrant, or high control both internally and externally—mutual creation. This quadrant represents the belief system of this book. We believe that all people can have significant influence over their own lives. We believe that we, as humans, can make a huge difference in creating our own lives, but that we are not gods. While we can make a difference in creating our lives, our environment can still play a large role in our ultimate success or failure. An innocent person being victimized by a drunk hit-and-run driver is not totally responsible for the outcome of what happened.

When we don't understand how much control we actually have in a given situation, it's easy to end up with misguided aspirations and inappropriate metrics. If we aren't careful, we can be pulled off course by going to either extreme—believing we can do everything or believing we control nothing. (For example, parents telling us that we are born winners who can do *anything* we choose—or parents telling us that we are born losers who can do *nothing* we choose.) Naively accepting their advice is forgivable in childhood, regrettable in early adulthood, and harmful in maturity.

As we become more successful, the importance of the top right quadrant grows, raising the bar still higher for responsible aspirations and metrics of improvement.

Applying the Right Criteria

Here's a brief test on your personal metrics and norms:

1. Choose someone you consider to be a personal hero. It could be someone from personal life experience, such as a parent or teacher, or someone in the news, such as Sully Sullenberger (who landed his disabled plane in the Hudson River with no loss of life).

2. Write the personal traits of this person that make you consider him or her to be a hero on the lines below. While you may not like everything about this person, think of at least three reasons that he or she is one of your heroes. These virtues could be patience, boldness, great use of language, and so forth.

   1. _____

   2. _____

   3. _____

3. Now return to step 1, cross off your hero's name, and write in your own name.

4. List which of the traits from step 2 you already possess and which you would like to develop.

   1. Possess: _____

      Need to develop: _____

   2. Possess: _____

      Need to develop: _____

   3. Possess: _____

      Need to develop: _____

   4. Possess: _____

      Need to develop: _____

The point of the exercise is that we can often control those traits that will make us "heroes"—emulating those we really admire for their deeds, behavior, and impact.

But we must become accustomed to an environment that we create and realize that this environment also influences us, a reciprocity of influence. Churchill, commenting on Parliament and its difficulties in taking action, said, "We shape our buildings, and afterwards, our buildings shape us."[2] What we're espousing is perhaps more of a

---

[2] Winston Churchill, House of Commons speech, 1944, quoted in *Learning Architecture* (blog), May 18, 2011, https://architectureintlprogram.wordpress.com/2011/05/18/.

halfway house, in which we build, digest, build, digest, alter, remove, build, digest, and so on.

The preceding exercise was designed by my (Marshall's) great friend Ayse Birsel.[3] It changed my life. As it turns out, all of my heroes were teachers. They included amazing leaders like Frances Hesselbein (Presidential Medal of Freedom award winner and former CEO of the Girl Scouts), Alan Mulally (2011 CEO of the Year in the United States and former CEO of Ford), as well as wonderful professors such as Peter Drucker and Warren Bennis. What did my heroes have in common? Not only were they fantastic coaches and teachers, they were extremely generous! None of my heroes ever charged me for any of the countless hours of help that they graciously gave to me. Although I have always thought of myself as a generous coach and teacher, I decided that I could do better. I decided to "adopt" 15 coaches and teach them all that I know for free—with the only price being that they would agree to pay it forward and do the same for others when they grew older.

I made a short video about my idea and posted it on LinkedIn. It went viral, and well over 100,000 viewers watched it. Over 12,000 people applied for the 15 positions! I decided to expand the project to include 100 established coaches and 100 aspiring coaches. I am happy to say that this is project is now a large part of my life, and I love it! (Thank you, Ayse Birsel, for this great exercise!)

The Impossible Dream

In the hit musical show *Man of La Mancha*, there is a moment only to be found on Broadway in which the character Don Quixote walks to stage center and everyone knows what's about to happen: The actor (I was fortunate enough to see Richard Kiley in the original production and Brian Stokes Mitchell more recently in the revival) sings "The

---

[3] Ayse Birsel, *Design the Life You Love* (Berkeley, CA: Ten Speed Press, 2015), www.amazon.com/Design-Life-Love-Step-Step/dp/1607748819.

Impossible Dream,"[4] a paean to the heroism of tilting at windmills. Some of the ideas expressed:

To fight those who were thought to be unbeatable
To bear more sorrow than seems bearable
To seek out areas where brave men don't dare tread
To reach the most distant star

You get the idea, and it's one hell of a theatrical moment. But it's not very helpful in setting or fulfilling your aspirations! Broadway musicals, like motivational seminars, can be inspiring—their intent is to immerse you in someone else's version of reality, with the hope that you'll be moved by the theatrics and grandeur in front of you.

Of course, there is nothing wrong with an enjoyable night at the theater, or spending a day or two at a motivational seminar—if it inspires you to live a better, happier, more thoughtful life. Many smart people with excellent intentions run these seminars, and in general they do more good than harm. The problem comes when we, the audience, rely on motivational experiences to give us all the answers. The fact is that these seminars can give us a lot—but not everything. The fundamental work of changing our behavior for the better is ultimately our own responsibility.

Cervantes invented Don Quixote, a character emblematic of people who believe they can do anything because of their deep belief. While people who believe "I can do it!" are more likely to do it, we have also seen many people delude themselves into thinking that a positive attitude can replace hard work. A great example of combining positive attitude and hard work occurred when NASA scientists saved the *Challenger*. They did not give up. They had a "We will do it!" attitude. They also had the years of training, the intelligence, and the dedication to make it happen. (I heard one of those engineers

---

[4] Mitch Leigh (composer) and Joe Darion (lyrics), "The Impossible Dream," from *Man of La Mancha* (play), 1965. (We can't publish exact song lyrics but we think you can recognize the gist!)

speak to a small group once holding a small piece of an O-ring. Now *that* was a motivational speech.)

A standard feature in old horror movies was the buzz saw that kept getting closer and closer to the hero. Although we knew the hero would somehow escape due to ingenuity, the arrival of the cavalry, or a *deus ex machina,* we still cringed.

Today we might cringe at the spinning wheel of social media, which is constantly gaining speed. We seek to be part of the latest, but there is so much "latest" that it's hard to stay constantly connected. We're driven to have the attention span of a water bug. We're immersed in an ADD world.

What has this to do with aspirations and metrics?

We may feel as if we don't exist if we're not a part of this spinning wheel of information. The centrifugal force threatens to throw us off, so we cling with all our might, trying to follow and be a part of a thousand issues for a second each. (Have you seen the Twitter members who "follow" 90,000 people? Try to follow even 25 daily and read their tweets, then add in the other social media platforms, and you have a full-time job.)

The inertia is bizarre: The more you get, the more you get! So we become overwhelmed with examples, advice, and claims that are never vetted, validated, or verified. At one point, people sold books and tapes through infomercials that showed how the average person could make millions by flipping houses or selling detergents. Pyramid and Ponzi schemes (sometimes politely called *multi-level marketing*) lulled people into the belief that they could make six figures by merely attracting people to become representatives of the organization selling phone cards or cleaning materials or breadboxes. Of course, the only people making real money were the authors of these schemes and the broadcasters.

Today, the phenomenon is multiplied a zillionfold with the unceasing, untiring, always increasing speed of the wheel of information that constantly spins in front of us. We don't *really* know what makes sense and what does not, what's real and what's a lie. If we are not careful, instead of becoming highly skeptical of most things, we can tend to accept almost *whatever is in front of us.*

As Daniel Kahneman, the Nobel Prize–winning behavioral economist noted, "What you see is all there is."[5] After all, experienced investment firms and government regulators for years accepted the ludicrous claims of huge returns in a down market from Bernie Madoff, who operated the most notorious of contemporary Ponzi schemes, and whose operation ruined tens of thousands of lives and careers.

Thus, our aspirations and goals are seldom purely our own. They are tainted or even created by the furious pace, noise, and general uproar around us—around the spinning wheel, the buzz saw. Why else would people watch scripted "reality" shows of little consequence?

We've lost our sense of perspective.

Life's Detours

Yogi Berra famously said that when you come to a fork in the road you should take it.[6] We know that's logically impossible, but we also know that the road of life is filled with unexpected twists and turns that can be terrific opportunities or harmful detours. It's easy to wander down interesting paths and alleys only to find that we don't know the way back. We wind up disoriented and lost in the wilderness of our own lives. We end up in a career, a location, or a relationship that is far from ideal—and struggle to get back.

To navigate our way home again, it helps to consider these detours. What pulls us away from our well-intentioned goals?

Family

Families are our first and strongest influences. They can help us become the people we want to be, but they can also send us on

---

[5] Daniel Kahneman, *Thinking, Fast and Slow* (New York: Farrar, Straus and Giroux, 2011), www.amazon.com/Thinking-Fast-Slow-Daniel-Kahneman/dp/0374533555/ref=sr_1_1?s=books&ie=UTF8&qid=1484684216&sr=1-1&keywords=thinking+fast+and+slow.

[6] Yogi Berra, *The Yogi Book* (New York: Workman Publishing, 1998).

detours—even when they mean well and are doing their best to help us. They model roles and behavior that we choose to adopt or reject later in life. Most of the time they have a strong influence on our education, determining where we go to school, including college. The rate at which children enter a family business or choose a parent's profession—or specifically reject it—is substantial.

Family experience also strongly influences:

- Perceptions of marriage fidelity, divorce, and relationship stability
- Use of drugs and alcohol
- Bias, prejudice, and ethics
- The sense of contribution and fairness
- Expectations of others

The same thinking can be applied to the social world outside our families. Our early exposure to social norms often determines how much attention we pay to education, authority, and responsible behavior. If we see our peers engaging in a certain behavior, we're far more likely to try it ourselves. That can be negative (when it comes to drugs or alcohol, for example) or positive (when we see peers succeeding academically or helping others).

Media

Social media presents unprecedented opportunities. It's given birth to inspiring social movements and empowered individuals to do great things. But it comes with huge challenges, too. Once, television was thought to be a dangerous influence, but it's mild compared to what we see on social media. Just as Pokémon's reality game causes traffic accidents when people pay attention only to the screen and not to the reality around them, the ongoing rush of news/gossip/video/innuendo/distraction on social media influences our choices—either from directives that are perceived (do this) or through passivity (ignoring what to do). We find ourselves in a cyclonic movement, a thrill ride, with issues and options hurtling around us along with the occasional chair or cow. It's hard to make sense of one direction or even to choose one.

Other digital technology surrounds us as well. Most of the time, it makes our working and our personal lives more convenient. But it also encroaches on our time. Unlike previous eras, the workday doesn't stop neatly at five o'clock for most professionals, so we're often struggling to finish up at home (and we can, thanks to technology). Combine that with the many digital distractions available to all ages, and it's hard to sit down and simply eat dinner as a family or talk over the day's events uninterrupted by electronic pinging and chirping.

Film and television still play a big role in shaping our consciousness too. With the advent of TV came a generation of kids who wanted to become astronauts, cowboys, and actors—like the heroes on their favorite shows. Today, TV is saturated with programming about how to achieve professional success in a series of glamorous careers— as chefs, fashion designers, house flippers, models, pop stars . . . and the list goes on. Our culture is obsessed with the notion that grit and big dreams are all it takes to succeed (lesson one in the school of purely internal control). Beating the odds to live a dream is such a common narrative that we all think we can do it—even when the odds are hugely stacked against the attempt. Just ask a server in any Los Angeles restaurant and he'll tell you the job is temporary until he gets his big break. A tiny percentage of these servers are right (so always tip handsomely, since you might have ordered your crème brûlée from the next George Clooney). But for the rest, every empirical piece of evidence demonstrates that they are servers who deny reality.

Given the pervasiveness of our media culture, how do you make a smart decision about what dreams and aspirations are really best for you? It can be hard to find time to stop and think.

Religious Institutions

While the United States remains one of the most religious countries in the world (by stated affiliation), religious participation in our country is steadily waning according to a study of 35,000 adults from the Pew Research Center: Religion and Public Life.[7] Scandals about child abuse in the Catholic Church—the largest single denomination in the United States—have driven people from the institution and undermined its message. The age of church attendees, based on casual observation, clearly skews close to 60. Religion is no longer the cultural bedrock it once was.

Business

There are plenty of heroes worth emulating in business today. But the business world changes so fast that knowing which successful person to follow can feel a little dizzying. Not only that, scandals in businesses from Enron to Volkswagen have undermined the role of business in creating standards and guidelines for behavior, careers, and aspirations. Too often, we see an "everyone-for-themselves" philosophy, exacerbated by business leaders doing perp walks in handcuffs to jail. (And the unanswered question: How many have gotten away with something and not been caught?)

Government

Politics, too, is an area characterized by rapid change and disruption. Just when we think we've got a grasp on how the system works, an election or a scandal upends our assumptions. Gone are the days of simple faith in authority. If anything is clear after the upheavals of the last few election cycles, it's that unpredictability may be the new normal.

Our main institutions—the family, the media, religion, business, and government—are in flux. While some of those changes are good, all of this volatility makes it hard for us to set aspirations and metrics for success. Without major institutions to guide us, where can we turn? The answer may be toward each other—to our friends.

---

[7] Pew Research Center: Religion and Public Life, "U.S. Public Becoming Less Religious," November 3, 2015, www.pewforum.org/2015/11/03/u-s-public -becoming-less-religious.

2 | The Importance of New Friends

Why Old Friends and Old Habits Tend to Stick Together

We tend to become the people who are our friends.

In many cases, that's a great thing. Both of us have been extremely fortunate in the friends we made early on in life. Without their support, we might not have gone on to have successful careers and happy lives. The relationships we've formed during our adult lives have also guided and inspired us in more ways than we can count. In this chapter, we'll make the case that building new relationships at every age is important. We'll also discuss those situations when a friend or a social group may be hurting us—and what to do about it. Humans are hardwired for loyalty and empathy. It can be hard to admit when a relationship is harmful. But it's ultimately helpful to all parties in a relationship to break a chain of negative influence.

To give a typical example, average weight in the United States has increased annually despite billions spent in the last decade alone on dietary supplements, medical interventions, exercise equipment, gym memberships, books, videos, retreats, and all manner of other attempts to lose mass. We laud self-discipline, brag about losing four pounds, and make *The Biggest Loser* into high-ratings TV.

But perhaps the obsession with weight ought to be viewed from a different perspective: We tend to be as heavy or as slim as most of our friends.

The ideal weight for people has increased commensurate with average weight, generally cited as about 10 pounds below prevailing averages. The fact that it, too, has risen demonstrates that it's simply more acceptable to be heavy today than it used to be. Why? Because so many more people are heavier than they used to be and than members of the general population ever were.

One study revealed that if your waiter is overweight, you will tend to order more food or overindulge.[1] In a sample of nearly 500 people, diners ordered more food—especially dessert—if the waiter were demonstrably heavy versus being thin. This was true irrespective of the diners' weight. The researchers said that diners seem to feel they had permission to indulge if being served by a heavy waiter.

It's tough to fight such normative pressure no matter how much exercise equipment and weight-watching groups you toss into the ring. I don't feel uncomfortable, awkward, or a standard deviation apart from you if we're both wearing extra large and there's more than one person also requiring the seat-belt extension on the airplane.

We support this with reality adjustors: A woman who once wore a size 14 dress now wears a size 10 because at the bottom end of the scale we have bizarre sizes like 0. We've skewed measurement to pretend that we're not heavy.

Guidepost

Some sociologists claim that many people who marry tend to look alike, and that they grow to look more identical over time during the marriage!

---

[1] Brian Wasnick, "11 Surprising Ways to Shed Pounds," Bottom Line, October 1, 2016, http://bottomlineinc.com/11-surprising-ways-shed-pounds.

Recidivism is quite high among ex-convicts, and readdiction quite high after rehab. When a drug abuser or alcoholic returns and hangs out with addicts and drinkers, the behavior resumes. It's extraordinarily difficult to resist what's going on around you among your peers. Hence, Alcoholics Anonymous insists on frequent meetings and sponsorships by peers *who are recovering and create a different norm.*

It's never a good bet to expect people to change a habit—any kind of habit—if they are surrounded by people voluntarily and happily engaged in that same habit. The default position is pretty clear: We tend to hang with people who are like us and live near people like us.

One of the great *New Yorker* cartoons depicted an employer interviewing a candidate across a desk, and both looked identical. The employer was saying something like: "I can't put my finger on it, but I really like what I see!"

Breaking Out of the "Good Enough" Trap

I (Marshall) have seen negative social pressure play out many times while coaching for behavioral change. I call this the "good enough" trap: We look around at the situation and say, "There's no need for me to keep trying so hard when the people around me are perfectly happy with mediocrity."

It's true that perfection is impossible, especially when it comes to behavior. Is anyone perfectly humble? Perfectly patient? A perfect listener? A perfect delegator? But we should keep striving to get better, or we risk losing our edge. In my experience, four environments trigger "good enough" behavior:

1. *We lack motivation:* If we don't really believe that the goal is worthy or that we lack the skill to do a task well, we shouldn't take it on. Find something that you care about and go after it with gusto.
2. *We're working pro bono, volunteering, or getting paid less than we think we should be:* Doing substandard work only reflects badly on us in the long run. Take the example of a restaurant owner who donates leftover food that is starting to spoil. She may

think she's doing the homeless a favor. Something is better than nothing, right? But all those needy people and their advocates will remember is bad food.

3. *We refuse to acknowledge our weaknesses:* We tend to see our strengths as our real qualities and our shortcomings as aberrations that don't really define us. We grow when we take responsibility for the whole package—good, bad, and in between.

4. *We have compliance issues:* No one likes to be told what to do— even (and sometimes especially) when the person telling us what to do is right. Saying we're "good enough" the way we are is a way to thumb our noses at authority.

Now, to be clear, "good enough" sometimes really is good enough! In many areas, there's no point in trying to be perfect. (Do we really need perfect mustard on our sandwiches, or a perfect score on a pass-fail test?) But when it comes to our interactions with others— how we treat each other—"good enough" sets the bar too low. Not only that, the payoff for *not* settling is tremendous. Pouring all of our energy into behavioral change means that we start to change our environment rather than be changed by it. Our forward progress is exciting and contagious, as others start to make changes in their lives, too. Imagine if one person in a group of overweight people really dedicates himself or herself to losing weight and keeping it off. It is harder to lose weight without the social support of a peer group, but once one person commits, others will find it easier. Pretty soon positive peer pressure begins to take hold.[2]

The Best Relationships Grow with Us

Maintaining old friendships is a wonderful thing. Keeping in touch with the people who knew us as children adds dimension to our lives and softens the passage of time. However, we don't recommend

---

[2] Marshall Goldsmith and Mark Reiter, *Triggers: Creating Behavior That Lasts— Becoming the Person You Want to Be* (New York: Crown Publishing, 2015).

having *solely* childhood friends. Getting to know new people is critical. The new (and newer) people in our lives reflect our changing selves, and they are a valuable part of our personal growth. Have you ever attended a high school or college reunion? It's an object lesson in the way friendships change over the years. It's fascinating to see your younger self reflected in the people around you. It's even better when old friends understand the person you've become. The strongest relationships are not set in amber like a prehistoric mosquito, frozen in time. They change with us.

While it's often quite difficult to retain friendships in a peripatetic world, social media makes it a simple task. On Facebook and Twitter, for example, our friends and followers never disappear, unless we choose to get rid of them.

We are contained within a peer group in virtual perpetuity. That can be constricting if we forget that on social media, as in real life, we are free to engage with or avoid people as we see fit. The problem comes when we let these old associations constrain our sense of identity.

Another huge challenge of our media-dominated environment is the way it encourages us to vicariously lead the lives of other people. Many who consider themselves more sophisticated than the rest of us mock the public neediness of Kim Kardashian and family. But Ms. Kardashian, et al., are pretty clever. They know there is a vast audience who wants to see their attention-seeking exploits. I don't know how else to describe Ms. Kardashian, who has no discernable talent other than being a great capitalist: She knows people want to watch and live their lives through her and her companions, so she makes herself highly accessible and controversial. Voilà: personal empire.

Scroll through your social media feed and you'll probably see a number of aspiring Kardashians: people exploiting their lives for attention or profit. They invite you to live vicariously through their ever-unfolding personal dramas—but beware of subordinating your own life to theirs. It's easy to be drawn into the world of celebrities, star athletes, or business executives—especially when they act in ways that shock us. But when you are old and gray and sitting in your rocking chair, will you look back with satisfaction on what the Kardashians did? No, you'll remember your own life—the people you loved and the mountains you climbed (literally or figuratively). Even the mistakes you made will be reason to celebrate, if they helped you to grow. The point is, they're your loves, your mountains, and your mistakes. No one else's.

Watertight Doors

As executive coaches and consultants, we work with many highly successful people. Very often, the behaviors and actions that made them successful aren't helping them anymore. (I, Marshall, wrote about this phenomenon in my bestselling book *What Got You Here Won't Get You There*.) For example, successful leaders have always been good at winning, but as they move up the organizational ladder they may have a tendency to win *too much*—when it matters, when it doesn't, and when it's completely beside the point. They are excellent at adding value, but they may now have an unfortunate tendency to add *too much* value, inserting their opinions into every discussion. Some other examples of this unhelpful behavior include passing judgment, making destructive comments, refusing to share information, advertising their own intelligence, and claiming credit they don't deserve, to name a few. Of course, everyone has these challenges, but the higher you go on the career ladder, the more peoples' problems tend to be behavioral. At high levels, everyone is smart, accomplished, and technically skilled. People skills are usually the key differentiator of success.

I (Alan) have coined (or appropriated) the term "watertight doors" to depict the phenomenon of behavior that is consistent with someone's current or former station in life. You can see this idea illustrated in Figure 2.1. It comes down to this: The higher we rise in life, the more we are responsible for helping others to rise through our daily behaviors and actions. People don't want to see us win, add value, be smart, or claim credit. We've already proved ourselves in those areas. Now our job is to help others show what they can do.

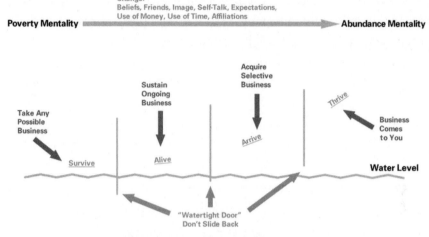

Figure 2.1 Watertight Doors

The first stage in the watertight-doors diagram is survival. We want to feed ourselves and our families, pay the mortgage or the rent, and create independent income. We tend to scrimp and to take any work that we can get. We don't engage in as much sharing or generosity because we're not in a position to give much.

We then progress to the stage of being alive. We have a sound position in a firm or have started our own business and are making money to cover expenses and put a little away.

Next we arrive. Our position or business is on a solid foundation and is growing. We have regular savings vehicles, take vacations, may send the kids to private school, and have low debt outside of a mortgage. We can be generous and participative. We are executives or successful entrepreneurs.

Finally, we thrive. We have large amounts of discretionary time and disposable income. We can be philanthropic. We may continue in our current professions or strike out into different pursuits. Our view of the world should be one of mutual creation (see Figure 1.1).

Yet what is all too often observed is someone with the *accoutrements* of the Thrive stage behaving as if at a lower level. What's required to seal those watertight doors, to batten them closed so that behaviors from past stages of our evolutionary journey don't slosh about inappropriately in our present lives? Conscious and disciplined change is required primarily in the following areas:

Beliefs: We find ourselves believing we're still outside after we've come inside. We may believe that working long hours is still a necessity to demonstrate that we're serious, whereas in reality working smart is now more important than working hard. We seldom raise our beliefs to the level of deliberate examination, yet beliefs create attitudes that inform our behaviors.

Image: Billy Joel does a great job in the song "Keeping the Faith" of explaining how image changes during maturity—you're no longer the big man just because you have on Cuban heels with smokes wrapped up in your shirt driving your old man's Chevrolet. But many never seek to change their image, which instead becomes a suit of armor protecting them from the onslaught of change.

Expectations: Aspirations change. We can't go through life successfully with constantly full and unmet bucket lists. We have to up our game. Mostly, we should expect to continue growing and not assume that we've reached our proper level. A lot of people around you arise in the morning and think, "This is it." This is the life they lead, as if life is a snapshot and not a movie. *You create your legacy every day, not at the end of your life.*

Case Study

When I (Alan) was promoted to head the San Francisco office of a global training firm, my wife and I accompanied a real estate agent to check out houses on Belvedere Island in Tiburon. I stopped, stock-still, in the great room of one of them, looking at a sweeping staircase, watching the bay through huge windows, with harbor seals barking in the background. My parents never had money, and it seemed surreal that I would even be able to consider buying a house like this.

"Is something wrong?" asked the Realtor, who realized I had stopped moving.

"Nothing wrong," I said, "it's just a bit dizzying when reality catches up with your aspirations."

Use of money: At certain times in our lives it's sensible to preserve cash, to let someone else pick up the check, to be practical. However, there comes a time when we should always offer to pick up the check, to be generous with others, to become philanthropic. The more we give in life, the more we get, and this becomes easy to do at the Thrive level. One of the great joys of becoming successful, for both of us, has been our ability to give to others and ask for little or nothing in return. I (Alan) am involved in many philanthropic activities. I (Marshall) donate my services frequently—including through my 100 Coaches program, which I described in Chapter 1.

Use of time: We need to reexamine time so that old habits, necessary evils, and a sense of obligation are largely abandoned. You can't reach out until you let go. You can't proceed to the next level while clinging to the last one.

Letting Go to Reach Out

Remember playground monkey bars? You were supposed to cross from one side of the structure to the other by just swinging by your arms. I (Alan) used to freeze until my knuckles were white and my arms were cramped and I dropped the thousand feet down (actually about two feet). But I saw, counterintuitively, that my friends who made it across let go with one hand to reach out, alternating until the momentum helped them traverse the monkey bars.

To reach upper levels and slam watertight doors shut, you have to let go before you can reach out.

> **Milepost**
>
> Contrary to what most people believe, money and time are not resources; they are priorities. We all have time and money, but the key differentiator is where we invest them. That means we don't have to gather more resources, but instead change our priorities as our conditions change.

Affiliations: It's generous—a trait we've lauded earlier—to belong to organizations and associations and invest our time, help others, and help good causes. However, even these have to be examined as candidates for change. Belonging to a chapter of an organization that focuses on speaking, or coaching, or influence might make sense as you progress in life, but you can outgrow these readily. In fact, some people stay on to become officers and board members and never leave, which means instead of raising the standard of the organization, the organization slows them down.

This is why, as a rule, we recommend that at a minimum you consider moving on from—or at least review your membership status in—mastermind groups and similar mutual-help arrangements every two years. Contrary to conventional wisdom, it's fine to be the most successful person in the group (someone has to be)—just not for too long! If your goal is self-improvement, it's probably time to find new challenges after two years.

Self-Talk: The field of positive psychology has made huge strides, offering among other insights that the way we talk to ourselves informs our behavior.[3] At earlier stages when someone doesn't react the way we wish we may say, "I'm a lousy marketer" or "I don't debate well." We generalize from a specific event, making it about character instead of the particular situation.

---

[3] The seminal work is perhaps *Learned Optimism* by Martin Seligman (New York: Vintage, 2006).

As we progress, we simply need to identify unsuccessful situations and learn from them (she didn't purchase my services today) and generalize victories, making them about character (an especially valuable device when raising children).[4] Some examples follow.

Specific	General
I made a nice sale.	I'm a great marketer.
I was convincing at the budget meeting.	I use influence well.
I was happy to contribute to this charity.	I'm generous.

Friends: And finally, friends. We've discussed the changes required to seal watertight doors, and some of those changes involve friends. We are close to many of our old friends, and we believe strongly in the value of loyalty. The true friend whom we can count on day and night, share secrets with, ask for advice, and gain support no matter what is not to be abandoned. However, we also believe we should be honest in assessing our friendships. Misery loves company, the old saying goes, and some friends need allies in their unhappiness. You do that person no favors by confirming his or her negativity. And you certainly don't help yourself. We're not suggesting that you ditch friends who need help or who are going through a rough patch. But there is such a thing as a toxic relationship, whether it's professional, between friends, or romantic. The closer you are to that person, that harder it is to disentangle yourself. In some cases it really is for the best to leave that person behind and move on.

One of the chronic problems for people who get promoted is that they have to treat prior peers as subordinates and prior superiors as peers. This can be far tougher than it seems. It

---

[4] Instead of "nice kick," say, "You're a terrific athlete." Instead of "good test score," say, "You're becoming a scholar."

requires a change in attitude, perspective, and reactions. Learning to relate to new peers eases the transition.

Why We Halt the Journey

Our journey is sometimes halted, suspended, detoured, or even abandoned. We may think there's someone in our way—as in the external
control we discussed in Chapter 1—but usually we've created the
obstacle in our own minds.

Part of the difficulty stems from poor self-talk:

I can't take the chance.
There's too much risk.
I'm overwhelmed.
I have no idea what to do.

Another obstacle is the rut we're in. Like cross-country skiers,
we're stuck in a set of tracks that someone else has created with a particular route in mind (becoming a lawyer, going to pharmacy school).
Or we find someone else ahead of us moving slowly, and there's no
way to pass *unless we leave the track and create our own path around the
obstacle, which requires strength, stamina, and most of all, intention.*

A third factor is procrastination (which is largely fear based): I'm
going to stop at the inn and continue the journey tomorrow. I'm
going to have a meal and get some sleep. I want to get off my track
because I heard of some great bird watching on another trail nearby.

Think of the times in your life you've observed people abandon
a project, give up for no reason, or invent excuses as to why they
couldn't continue. Have you ever scoffed at them for being so weak,
for having no perseverance, for not possessing resilience? Of course,
when you've chosen to abandon the journey there have been perfectly
good reasons, right?!

The evolutionary journey from surviving to thriving requires a
sort of global positioning system. You have to identify the next steps,
recognize the next level, and understand how to seal the doors behind
you. We are often slowed because we're expecting people to keep up
with us rather than finding friends who force us to speed up. We take

our time because we're comfortable, having feathered a nest that we're not willing to leave.

The journey is one that proceeds *from* a poverty and scarcity mentality *toward* an abundance mentality. This isn't about money, it's about beliefs and behavior. The reason some people with a comfortable life still act as they did when they weren't so comfortable isn't force of habit. It's the belief that what they have is scarce and perhaps temporary: I'm doing well today, but what if I'm not doing as well tomorrow?

I (Marshall) always try to operate from a place of abundance and generosity. As an executive coach, I have a unique compensation system—I only get paid if my clients get better. "Better" means my clients achieve positive, measurable change in behavior, not as judged by themselves but by their key stakeholders. This process usually takes about 18 months and involves an average of 16 stakeholders.

My coaching approach has been described in several major publications, including *Forbes* and the *New Yorker*. I have been asked many times where I came up with this "pay only for results" idea. The answer is Dennis Mudd, who installed a new roof on my family's home in Valley Station, Kentucky, when I was growing up. My family was poor. Dad operated a small, two-pump gas station. The roof on our home was very old and starting to leak badly. We had no choice but to get a new roof, although it was a painful expenditure for us. Dad hired Dennis Mudd to put on the roof. In order for us to save some money, I worked as his assistant.

Putting on a roof in the middle of the summer in Kentucky is incredibly hard work. I never have done another job (before or since) that required this degree of physical exertion. I was amazed at the care Mr. Mudd put into the laying of the shingles. He was patient with me as I made mistakes and helped me learn how to do the job right. After a while, my attitude toward this project changed from grudging acceptance to pride in a job well done. In spite of the heat and pain, I looked forward to working with Mr. Mudd every day.

When the project was finally over, I thought the roof looked great. When Mr. Mudd presented my dad with the invoice for our work, he said quietly, "Bill, please take your time and inspect our work. If you feel that this roof meets your standards, pay us. If not, there is no charge for our work." It was obvious he was very serious in his request.

Dad carefully looked at the roof, thanked both of us for a job well done, and then paid Dennis Mudd, who then paid me for my help.

I will never forget watching Dennis Mudd when he told Dad to only pay for results. He wasn't kidding—he was dead serious, and my already high respect for Mr. Mudd skyrocketed. I was only 14 years old, but I will never forget this event. I knew the Mudd family. They didn't have any more money that we did. I thought, "Mr. Mudd may be poor, but he is not cheap. This guy has class. When I grow up, I want to be like Dennis Mudd."

Although I have received many honors for my work, I doubt I will ever match the dedication to quality and the integrity Dennis Mudd showed. Mr. Mudd taught me a lesson that I will try to live up to for the rest of my life. What is important is not how much he impressed me. What is much more important is that he could look with pride at the person he saw in the mirror every day.

If every leader in business and government operated like Dennis Mudd, the world would surely be a better place. Imagine if everyone were willing to put pride in their work over financial exigencies. That is a remarkable example of the abundance mentality. Following are some examples of the differences between a scarcity mentality and an abundance mentality on the job and in the office, with colleagues and with subordinates.

Scarcity	Abundance
Create bureaucracy.	Do the right thing.
Are insecure.	Are self-confident.
See "them and us."	See "us."
Focus on task.	Focus on result.
Follow rules.	Think.
CYA.	Take risks.
See win/loss issues.	See win/win issues.

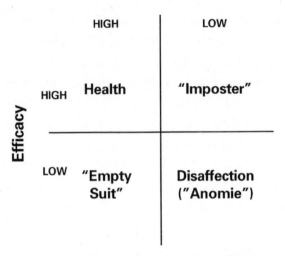

Figure 2.2 Esteem and Abundance

You can see by these examples that a scarcity mentality tends to create rules and constraints, the antithesis of freedom and autonomy. Yet autonomy is one of the key motivators in the workplace. Doing the right thing often means investing more time, taking more creative actions, and going beyond the rule book.

Confidence is required to maintain such values. Figure 2.2 shows another way to look at our control dynamics from Figure 1.1.

People who possess high self-esteem (feel worthy) are efficacious and healthy. But if you are good at what you do but don't really believe it (upper right of Figure 2.2), you believe you're going to be "caught," and await the eventual day or reckoning. People in this quadrant are "imposters." Dr. Pauline Rose Clance wrote about this phenomenon many years ago, having interviewed celebrities, business executives, athletes, and others who believed that some day they would be "found out."[5]

The lower left quadrant represents the "empty suit," where efficacy is low but esteem is very high: big promises but little delivery. And the bottom right is disaffection and alienation.

---

[5] Pauline Rose Clance, *The Imposter Phenomenon* (Atlanta: Peachtree Publishers, 1985).

Returning to our examples of scarcity versus abundance thinking, a scarcity mentality sees life as a zero-sum game. For me to win, you have to lose. If you win, I lose. (We all know people who aren't content with merely winning; the other person has to also clearly lose.) It requires abundance thinking to realize that I am enhanced by your victories, not diminished. Generosity necessitates such a win/win value system, which means that you have to believe there are more than sufficient positive outcomes and rewards for us all (and that you should join in the communal victories, not merely the personal ones).

Frankie Valli and the Four Seasons

Scarcity focuses on the task, not the larger result. This is a common issue with many consultants I coach who insist on implementing the six-step sales process with clients, rather than just leaping to the result when it's clearly in sight! Following a map when you can see the destination in front of you doesn't make a lot of sense unless you're afraid to believe your own eyes.

A scarcity mentality follows rules; an abundance mentality takes prudent risk. The former seeks comfort in the prescribed route, the latter often in the conventionally prescribed place. The reasons that one attorney can win exactly the same case that another loses is that the loser adheres strictly to the law and the rules while the winner sees the law in shades of gray wherein creativity and originality have roles (otherwise, why have judges and juries?).

At times on our journey we have to sever what seemed like unbreakable relationships and inseparable bonds. That's a necessity of change. Conditions change and circumstances are altered.

There is a famous, true story about Frankie Valli, the great lead singer of the legendary Four Seasons, and Bob Gaudio, another member of the group who wrote the songs.[6] Early in their careers

---

[6] The members of the Four Seasons are the subjects of the global hit musical *Jersey Boys*.

they shook hands and agreed to share whatever each one made fifty-fifty, regardless of who generated what. Eventually, Gaudio left the group to focus solely on composing, the group's members changed several times, and Valli went on to a solo singing (and acting) career.

Nevertheless, they continued to share according to the agreement of their twenties well into their seventies. The *business agreement* endured, but they went their separate ways in their careers. They remained friends, but they didn't remain friends based on joint membership in a musical group. They allowed themselves the freedom to go their separate ways.

3 | Behavioral Metamorphosis

Making Deliberate Change

It's not sufficient to have aspirational ideals. We need focused, targeted behaviors to support the journey toward that moving target. That's why we believe that everyone needs structure and support—in some cases from a coach who can honestly assess shortcomings and come up with a plan for improvement.

There is a reason that coaching has grown by leaps and bounds in the corporate world over the last few decades. Instead of a sign that a person's career is faltering, having a coach is now most often a mark of prestige—a signal that the company is making an investment in that person. For many people, it's harder to accept the guidance of a coach outside the workplace. Without the ego-soothing assurance that our coach is grooming us for future professional success, we are far more likely to take the coach's directives personally. Partly it's about a need for privacy. It's socially acceptable to admit that we could be more patient at work or that we could lose a few pounds. It's embarrassing and difficult, for example, to face our shortcomings as parents and as husbands or wives.

Sometimes we don't know that we need to change. We are in denial, convincing ourselves that others need help, not us. A few years ago, a large equipment company hired me (Marshall) to coach the CEO and the COO, who was to succeed the CEO in the near future. The CEO had a precise timetable for succession. "My number two is a good guy," he said, "but he needs three more years of seasoning. Then I'll be ready to leave, he can take over, and everything's good." My antennae perk up whenever I'm asked to conduct research that proves someone's predetermined conclusion. Something wasn't right. Sure enough, when I finished my 360-degree interviews with the COO's colleagues, they all said the number two was ready now. The deeper problem was the CEO. Without prompting, nearly every interviewee said the CEO had stayed too long and should leave for the good of the company.

Another important reason for acknowledging the support coaching provides: We have an inherent tendency to *underestimate* the difficulty required to accomplish any but the simplest of tasks (and sometimes even those). On a systemic basis, do you find that most bridge repairs, highway projects, new construction, and mass transit improvements are completed below budget or over budget, ahead of time or late? The "Big Dig" in Boston—a huge public works project that rerouted roads to run underneath the city and constructed a new route to the airport—was projected to cost $2.8 billion and was completed *nine years late* at a cost of $14.6 billion (that's 400 percent over budget). The cost was about twice the cost of building the Panama Canal in today's dollars![1]

But let's get past airports and space stations and focus on new desks for the local school, or installing a new kitchen in your home. As Roseanne Roseannadanna (Gilda Radner) was fond of saying on *Saturday Night Live*, "It's always *something*."

---

[1] "Big Dig," Wikipedia, last modified February 4, 2017, https://en.wikipedia.org/wiki/Big_Dig.

On a very personal basis, we tend to think that washing the car or having a quick lunch or walking the dog will take whatever time we assign to it. But as a transmogrification of Parkinson's Law, we often see that time expands to accommodate underestimated effort.[2] That's the reciprocal.

We are a culture that is adept at rejecting help in the pursuit of change. There is a certain shame attached to the option, akin to feeling you have mismatched socks at a formal dinner or that you have lettuce (today, perhaps kale) stuck in your teeth. The best of the best often have coaches—and many have more than one. But under that level of performance, there is a tropism toward a stubborn independence, a refusal to create dependence.

It's part of the successful person's unshakable self-sufficiency: We think we can do it all on our own. Quite often we can, of course. But what's the virtue in saying no to help? It's a needless vanity, a failure to recognize change's degree of difficulty. We both know this through long professional and personal experience. I (Marshall) have to pay a woman named Kate to call me every night to follow up on how I'm doing on my main priorities in life! This isn't professional hypocrisy, as if I'm a chef who won't eat his own cooking. It's a public admission that I'm weak, like everyone else, and need help. We all need help for something. The process of change is hard! Why not grab all the help we can get?

Not only that, the mistaken notion that we can independently cure what ails us adds to the disproportionate time required to change through trial and error, or, ultimately, the time required to search for and find the right help after we realize that we can't tell the difference among our socks.

When change takes so long, we tend to miss the best opportunities or solutions. We don't obtain the travel plan we most desire, we miss the tickets for the big event, we find someone else has beaten us to market, we spend more time on the issue than we really needed to.

---

[2] C. Northcote Parkinson, *Parkinson's Law or the Pursuit of Progress* (London: John Murray Publishers, 1958).

That's why abrupt change may make sense in some situations but a metamorphosis might be right for others. When the late, famed paleontologist Stephen Jay Gould of Harvard had trouble explaining some gaps in the evolutionary trail, he (and others) developed a theory called "punctuated equilibrium," wherein species make a leap instead of a gradual progression to a new form.[3] This may apply to our own lives in various forms.

Case Study

There are myriad approaches—from drugs to gum to support groups to hypnosis—to try if someone wants to stop smoking but cannot independently.

Both my father and father-in-law were heavy smokers. Their clothes and hair smelled of tobacco almost all the time. In the 1960s, when early health warnings began to appear (and those television doctors with their advice on the healthiest cigarettes disappeared), both of them quit—cold turkey.

They both said that they realized they should stop and simply did one morning, and never regressed. Surely, not everyone can do that; some require much more help, and some never succeed. But it does illustrate that achieving even radical change can vary greatly by individual.

The problem, of course, is that the best of coaches can't help anyone who doesn't want to be helped. So the fiercely independent are hard to reach (hence the occasional interventions staged by friends and family, which have varying degrees of success). Thus change is delayed by what may be fine intentions, and an unwillingness, at best, to impose on others—and, at worst, to expose one's vulnerabilities. And not all change attempts are appropriate for rapid help and quick resolution.

---

[3] Stephen Jay Gould, *Punctuated Equilibrium* (Cambridge, MA: Harvard University Press, 2007).

Unlike the rare successful cold turkey approach to stopping smoking, most people can't end 30-year habits overnight. *We all need help.* Finding the courage to want to change a habit is one thing, but having the courage to proactively reach out and seek help is quite another. Thinking we can do it all ourselves, that we don't want to show our vulnerabilities or failures to others, more often creates a powerful momentum for failure, to the point that when we even consider change we reflect that we haven't been able to do it the last six times we tried. So, why try it again?

I (Marshall) often ask the people in my seminars how long they have been trying to change a particular behavior. The answers usually run in years or even decades. I tell them, "You haven't made this change in 20 years! If you could have done it by yourself, you would have done it by now. Get some help."

Sometimes this help arrives in the form of a coach. Sometimes it comes from some other outside entity—a well-meaning friend or colleague. In the latter case, we often don't recognize it as help (Why is she telling me this?) or resent it (That was mean) or reject it (That's not what I said). It's hard to persist when you are constantly being rebuffed in attempting to help someone *because it becomes abundantly clear that you cannot help someone who doesn't want to be helped.*

In my (Marshall's) coaching business, I have learned that some people may say they want to change, but that they don't really mean it. They don't want to do the hard work of getting confidential feedback, apologizing for sins in the past, involving colleagues on a regular basis, and spending about a year and a half following up. With my colleague Howard Morgan, I conducted a very large research study with 86,000 people, called Leadership Is a Contact Sport. Our research clearly shows that leaders who don't do the work and don't follow up don't get better. So trying to coach these people is a bad investment for them, for the company, and for me. A sincere willingness to try has to be a minimum consideration.[4]

---

[4] Marshall Goldsmith and Howard Morgan, "Leadership Is a Contact Sport," *Strategy + Business* 36 (August 25, 2004) (originally published by Booz & Company), www.strategy-business.com/article/04307?gko=a260c.

I (Alan) was trying to help a colleague who was far too heavy, to the extent that it was negatively impacting his business. When you sat next to him you could hear his breathing. He wasn't comfortable in most seating arrangements and couldn't hold a laptop computer on his lap. After many discussions, and his sworn agreement to make changes, I still watched him eat the same awful foods and refuse to work out. Finally, a mutual friend, who had been similarly engaged in attempting to help, said to me, "That's it. We've tried. He won't change, he doesn't really want to. There's nothing more to be done." Today, he's heavier than ever, and his attitude has become vindictive and bitter. That's not where any of us want to wind up. So what do we do for positive change?

Ugly Caterpillars and Uglier Butterflies

Not all butterflies are beautiful, and not all caterpillars are ugly.

Metamorphosis is not a guarantee of a brighter and better future. Following are five questions to ask yourself to ensure that you methodically create a better future:

1. What behaviors do I seek to change?
2. What behavior will I substitute?
3. What assistance do I need to help with the change?
4. What metrics will tell me I'm making progress?
5. What will I do to sustain the change?

As an example, let's suppose you wanted to change your current behavior of becoming stressed and argumentative when something adverse occurs:

1. I want to change from feeling out of control, defensive, and slighted when someone does something that adversely affects me.
2. I want to be able to understand whether the other person's behavior was intentional or unintentional and react

appropriately—seeking understanding if the latter, and confronting the person positively and calmly if the former.

3. I need to take a breath before I speak or act and I need time to process the situation. To do that, I'll need to have a coach who can teach me the proper technique and/or whom I can consult when the situation arises.

4. I'll stop getting into arguments, stop feeling so stressed that I need to take antacid pills, and will be able to carry out the appropriate actions so that the situation is in my favor.

5. I'm going to practice not reacting to adverse information or behavior in the moment, to step away if it's an in-person encounter and to refrain from sending an email or making a call if it's a remote interaction. I will ask my partner to help me on an ongoing basis.

Most studies have found that it's very difficult to merely change poor behavior. It's much more effective to substitute a more positive behavior. If smoking provides oral pleasure, try chewing gum. If you break into others' commentary at work, take notes to use when they're done. In other words, retain the reward, but replace the bad behavior with more positive and beneficial behaviors.

Change for its own sake makes little sense, for organizations or individuals. The key is to determine the salutary results that make the change worthwhile. In the preceding example, preserving relationships, not becoming ill, not wasting time, and feeling more in control are all positive aspects of the change.

Another way to look at positive change is to examine your belief system. Beliefs create attitudes, which manifest in behaviors, as illustrated by Figure 3.1.

If we believe that no one under the age of 30 can perform in a certain job, our attitude will be contemptuous and our behavior will be dismissive. If we believe that teachers can provide us with the learning we need to succeed in the years ahead, our attitude will be attentive and our behavior will be respectful.

What we believe—about the police, the system, coworkers, ourselves, or anything else—creates the attitudes that inform our

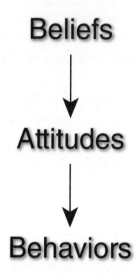

Figure 3.1   Manifestation of Beliefs

behavior. In our journey of change, of lifestorming, we need to constantly examine our belief systems before we engage in arbitrary behavior change. If you *believe* that spiders are dangerous or that you'll die in an airplane or that your boss hates you, you'll behave accordingly with flight, avoidance, and antipathy. This will occur no matter what training or coaching is assigned or undertaken.

There is an underlying belief system, often unarticulated, that causes flight, fight, and fright. Therapists seek to bring hidden beliefs to the surface. But those causes can often be examined by all of us while in thoughtful introspection.

Bad behaviors are too often dealt with through coercion: fines, chastisement, and punishments. But in most cases they are improved only so long as the punishment is present. People revert to comfortable or preferred behaviors once the big stick disappears. There are people who have received three speeding tickets while on the same trip, and kids who go back to their video games hidden under the covers after being threatened. The trouble with coercion is that it is ineffective once it is removed and often causes intensified bad behavior in retaliation.

Bad attitudes are generally dealt with through peer pressure: Don't be the only one not joining us. Be a team player. But norms are fickle and can readily change. The team can go rogue.

The best route to behavior change is an appeal to rational self-interest by appealing to and/or changing one's belief system. This is usually the intent of nonviolent protests. It's what whistleblowers try to create. And it's why education about smoking-related deaths has decreased tobacco use far more than draconian taxation. Most people can pay a little bit more for cigarettes. They can't abide the idea that they won't live to see their grandchildren grow up.

Metabehavior

Our behaviors need to change on our journey, both for the long haul and in the short term. We need help with both. Acknowledging that need and obtaining that help are signs of health and internal control.

The shortest period of needed change is situational, in the moment, now. We face an unexpectedly rude buyer, or an outraged colleague, or a key source who missed the deadline critical to your progress. Our reactions here are often the wrong default:

- We become angry and lash out.
- We blame ourselves and become despondent.
- We are shocked into silence and lose all control.
- We become confused and make poor decisions.
- We are shocked and retreat from the situation.
- We seek blame and cause others who can help us to retreat.

These behaviors are all dysfunctional. They exacerbate a deteriorating situation. They include many bad assumptions and attitudes, for example:

- This person can help me but won't.
- I must apply more volume or threat.
- I have to radically change my plans and expectations.

- I'm wrong in this pursuit.
- I've been misled.
- I've failed.

What if our belief system were such that our default position is that no one is damaged (which seems to be the very belief inherent in many self-help activities)? What if we believed that honest errors are human and natural, and that even deliberate inappropriate behavior is not intended to penalize us specifically? (The jerk who cut us off in traffic is simply a jerk who cuts off cars, who didn't mean it specifically as an affront to us. Or even better: What if we forgave his careless action on the assumption that he just didn't notice our car, as we occasionally have made the same error?)

I (Marshall) often share the following Buddhist parable in my seminars. It's about learning how to respond well when confronted with problems.

A young farmer paddled his boat vigorously upriver. He was covered with sweat as he paddled his boat upstream to deliver his produce to the village. It was a hot day, and he wanted to make his delivery and get home before dark. As he looked ahead, he spied another vessel heading rapidly downstream toward his boat. He rowed furiously to get out of the way, but it didn't seem to help.

He shouted, "Change direction! You are going to hit me!" The boat came straight toward him anyway. It hit his boat with a violent thud. The young man cried out, "You idiot! How could you manage to hit my boat in the middle of this wide river?"

As he glared into the boat, seeking out the individual responsible for the accident, he realized that there was no one. He had been screaming at an empty boat that had broken free of its moorings and was floating downstream with the current.

The interesting thing is that we behave one way when we believe that there is another person at the helm. We blame that stupid, uncaring person for our misfortune. We get angry, act out, assign fault, and play the victim. In other words, we are not engaged in a positive way but in a negative and defensive way that makes nothing better!

We behave more calmly when we know that what is coming toward us is an empty boat. With no available scapegoat we don't get upset. We make peace with the fact that our misfortune was the result of fate or bad luck and we do our best to rectify the situation. We may even laugh at the absurdity of a random unmanned boat finding a way to collide with us in a vast body of water.

The challenge for all of us is to recognize that there is often no one in the other boat. We are screaming at an empty vessel. An empty boat isn't targeting us. And neither are all the people who upset us over the course of a day. Treating all boats as empty forces us to accept what is and change what we can (and make peace with what we cannot change).

The empty boat story is one example of how, by changing our beliefs over the long haul, we're better able to deal with short-term disruptions in a healthy and productive manner.

Those disruptions might include a client who is surprisingly rude. In my (Alan's) experience, you can take it personally, retaliate, or just inquire: "You seem upset. Have I done something to inadvertently offend you?" That's a statement of observation (which may be corrected) and a question (which has to be answered). This reaction places you on the high road.

If a colleague informs you that your actions with a mutual client have undermined her plans for potential business, you might argue the point, or claim innocence, or ignore the claim. However, you can also apologize and respond, "I had no idea, I'm sorry, how can I help you retrieve the opportunity? Would you like some suggestions? I can call the client right now if it helps." If your colleague doesn't respond to such entreaties, then her own belief system is undermining her, not your actions.

Situational change can be the most difficult, because there often is no precedent for a given situation. It's usually a surprise and unanticipated, and it's very dependent on environment and the disposition of the people involved. That's why situation change tends to be so different in the office versus at home. And so a brief digression follows.

The secret to long-term successful marriages is to accept discord. When you live together you come to recognize situational change requirements. If you don't, you're not going to live together for too long, unless you're a masochist.

Case Study

I had a friend, a consultant and psychologist, no less, who had been married and divorced three times. He was almost always with a different woman, from a graduate assistant 20 years younger to an heiress 10 years older.

During one business trip, which included partners, he announced that he and his current flame were breaking up— *during the trip.*

"What happened?!" I asked.

"We had an argument about where to go for dinner, and that was that."

"An argument?"

"Yes. You two must never argue."

We were stunned and said, "Only about three times daily."

"And you're still together??"

"That's *why* we're together!

The ability to argue, disagree, and confront *when coupled with the ability to understand the dynamics of a disagreement, to not seek retribution, and to identify the need for reconciliation* are the underpinnings of long-term personal relationships. This is analogous to all relationships.

End of digression.

To progress from rejection of change to positive acceptance of change to deliberate creation of change is a healthy evolutionary journey. We lack the basis and precedent of long-term relationships in most of our situational relationships, but we can nevertheless apply healthy beliefs that create positive attitudes, which manifest in effective behavior.

Don't assume the boss is an ill-tempered, tone-deaf tyrant. Don't assume that every misfortune—including airplane delays due to weather—are sleights aimed specifically at you by perverse gods. Stop thinking you're misunderstood. Instead, talk to the boss about your issues or his or her communications, create alternative travel arrangements as your plan B in advance, go to lengths to make yourself understood, and then test to see if you were.

Here's a quick lesson about empowerment: It does you no good to argue with anyone who hasn't the capacity (authority, resources, and skills) to help you. Screaming at the client service phone agent because your package hasn't been delivered doesn't do anything except *decrease* the likelihood that the person being screamed at will help you to any extent at all. You need to find a level of management with the authority to help and then provide the manager with the incentive to help. When my baggage fails to arrive on occasion (I—Alan—have nearly 4 million air miles), I don't scream at the baggage agent in the tiny airport office. I say, "I know you deal with this all day long, so what can I do to best help you find my lost luggage?"

Case Study

I (Marshall) also travel a lot. Every time I hear the announcement that the plane will be late, I remember a picture in my library—a picture of me on a volunteer trip to Africa with the Red Cross when I was about 30 years old. The picture shows me with many starving children. Their arms are being measured. If their arms are too big they do not eat. If their arms are too small they don't eat. Their arms have to be just the right size—meaning they are not so hungry they won't survive and not so well fed as not to need food—to eat that day.

This was an eye-opening experience for me that I never want to forget. It reminds me how fortunate I am. When I feel "justifiably" upset, I remember that photo and those beautiful children. I repeat this mantra over and over in my mind: "Never complain because the airplane is late. There are people in the world who have real problems. They have problems you cannot even begin to imagine. You are a very lucky man. Never complain because the airplane is late." Next time that you board an airplane, and you hear the announcement that the airplane is going to be late, say to yourself, "I am such a lucky person."

Conversely, organizations that are on top of their game *empower* people at lower levels to help people, obviating the need to involve layers of management, which is redundant and actually expensive failure work. If front-line people have the authority to help customers who behave appropriately so as to merit their help, then we have highly effective resolutions.

Here's a key technique: When someone justifiably complains to you about something, merely ask, "What would make you happy?" Inevitably, they will ask for *less* than you would have provided on your own! (This is why Ritz-Carlton wisely—or at parent Marriott's wise insistence—changed its policy of providing virtually all employees with the authority to spend up to $2,500 on a guest complaint. Employees were offering more than they had to—say, a free night—when a simple free drink or just an apology would have sufficed.)

Our belief system needn't be that every discomfited customer or client is outraged, or that they want the moon and the stars to assuage their grievances. I've had drinks spilled on me on an airplane, and I forgave the passenger or flight attendant who did it. I didn't assume that they were sloppy or incompetent, because I know it was simply an accident.

Stuff happens. We need to deal with it in real time.

Aspiration-Appropriate Behavior

Our aspirations shouldn't be static. They are a moving target, not something to be accomplished and done with. As we move through our evolutionary journey, our aspirations change. We no longer seek to be in the major leagues, but to be an All-Star; to move from charitable giving to starting a philanthropy; from taking yearly vacations to traveling the world; from being a valued employee to starting our own business.

The options that pertain to most of us look like this:

1. Discretionary and deliberate change.
2. Change is acceptable.
3. Change is resisted.

At the lowest level, we've feathered a nest and don't want to budge. Change is threatening, so we resist external influences. While it's understandable that some people want to hang onto what they have, this position doesn't help them in the long run. In business, and in organizational culture more broadly, change is a constant—especially now, at a time when disruption and volatility are rapidly becoming the new normal.

Case Study

Imagine living a life in which nothing changed. I (Marshall) think it's great to keep some things the same all your life: your spouse, even a job or the community where you live. But if we live completely changeless lives, we miss out—especially if we hang onto poor habits, grudges, personal inertia, or something else that hurts others and ourselves. This amounts in the end to choosing misery.

So, if there is one thing I'd ask of you right now, it's to think about one change, one gesture that you won't regret later on. That's the only criterion: You won't feel sorry you did it! Maybe it's calling your mother to tell her that you love her. Or thanking a customer for his loyalty. Or, instead of saying something cynical in a meeting, saying nothing.

It could be anything, as long as it represents a departure from what you've always done and would continue to do forever if you hadn't read these words.

Now do it.

It will be good for your friends. It will be good for your company. It will be good for your customers. It will be good for your family.

And it will be even better for you. So much better that you might even want to do it again.

We can't merely expect to retrain and reskill. We need to change our beliefs about accepting change. That leads us to level two.

Here, we are receptive to change. The key to success here is an A+ attitude:

Accept: Accept the change without resistance or argument, so long as it doesn't threaten your ability to perform and succeed. (It usually doesn't.) Understand what's required and make intelligent, rational decisions, whether it's relocation, more schooling, different work, or changed relationships.

Adjust: Make the required changes in your habits and activities. Once you accept that the change can be in your self-interest, adjust your attitudes to allow for more flexibility, different options, and new conditions.

Adapt: Now your behaviors can change appropriately. Make new friends, end unhelpful relationships, choose different working habits, and spend your time in different ways. Become innovative in making the change work for you (the combination of internal and external control).

Once we've accepted that change happens, we can begin to think about how to bring about the changes we want. Thus, level three is about initiating change and exerting more internal control.

If our aspirations don't stop with a certain job title or mountaintop, then how are they created and managed during our journey? A caterpillar receives a biochemical indicator, or senses a weather change, or has an internal clock that informs it when to spin the cocoon. We have no such automated systems. We need to create our own triggers toward metamorphosis on our journey.

There is no best time to do this. But we do have to grapple with the disinclination to do it, the procrastination impulse, the feathered nest syndrome. We hear bromides such as "Don't undertake too much change at once," or "Stabilize your life before you consider more changes."

Ironically, a gyroscope remains upright only so long as it continues to spin.

We aren't in a snapshot; we're part of a film. We deal with what is today, knowing that it shouldn't necessarily be what is tomorrow. When we talk about aspiration-appropriate behavior, we mean adjusting behavior to deal with the moving target of enhanced aspirations. And that means adjusting our belief systems to support those newly desirable behaviors.

Write a belief you've had for quite some time and haven't changed and don't intend to change.

Now write a belief you once held and one that has replaced it.

Finally, project a new belief you might hold in the future.

For me, the first might have been:

I believe in freedom of the press and that the press should be objective and nonbiased.

For the second:

I once believed that a corporate job was best, and that you worked hard and that talent was recognized and promoted, but now I believe that I'm better off working for myself.

And for the third:

I well might come to believe that the current, two-party system needs to change to allow for more diverse candidates and opinions.

Figure 3.2   The Permission Gauge

You can see how our beliefs are sometimes constant, sometimes altered, and sometimes enhanced by new ones. We've found that one of the most important elements in this journey is allowing ourselves permission.

In position one, in the lower left of Figure 3.2, you assume you never have permission. You don't cross against the light even when you can see there's no traffic for a mile. You don't contradict a buyer, no matter how egregious the error. You would never ask a desk clerk for an upgrade, or duck under the endless ropes to make quicker progress toward the entrance. You never push back. You do not, ever, break from precedent. You have no editor, only a go/no go choice, which is usually shut down.

In position two, in the upper left, you formally ask. You ask your partner if it's okay to write a check for something from your joint account. You ask a client if you can talk to people as you travel through the site. You raise your hand and never just ask your question. You wait to see if someone else does what you want to do first, as a precedent.

You constantly ask others to approve your approach, proposal, article, and breakfast choice. You ask others to edit your work.

In position three, in the upper right, you formally grant yourself permission. You review the situation and affirm for yourself that it's okay to knock and enter the room. You say to yourself, "Well, they wouldn't have offered if they didn't want me to use it." You compare your work to others to ensure that you're on the right track. You justify and validate internally why it's okay to proceed. You might not break new ground, but you take advantage of ground already broken by others. You self-edit.

In position four, in the lower right, you simply assume permission. With the right ethical bearing, you don't commit antisocial behavior, such as cutting a line, but you go to the elite members' hotel lounge and assume you're entitled to because you have a large suite. You tell your client when, based on your criteria, there's been a bad decision. You ask a question without asking to be acknowledged first. You realize that some rules and even laws are situational and you use good judgment to guide your behaviors. You have neither an external nor an internal editor.

You may have realized that, as you go around the dial, you move through unconscious incompetency, conscious incompetency, conscious competency, and unconscious competency.

We think that the ideal setting for most people is between positions three and four. Based on three decades of working with all kinds of people across many industries, we know how common it is to operate between two and three.

The healthiest people, and those most in control of their journey, operate between positions three and four, on the right of Figure 3.2. They know at times they do require permission (I can't steal my sister's car) and at times they can simply act (She's away at school and the car needs to be driven).

Our behavioral metamorphoses—plural—take place purposefully over time. Let's now take a look at what determines the actual nature of our behaviors—our belief system.

4 | Believe It or Not

Breaking into the Belief Vault

Thomas Jefferson wrote, "We hold these truths to be self-evident."
This immortal sentence from the Declaration of Independence is
worth examining for a lot of reasons—notably, what exactly makes
a truth self-evident? What can we be sure is true, and what should we
question? Especially as we age, it's easy for beliefs to become so cal-
cified in our unconscious that we never revisit them, never question
them, and never change them. In this chapter, we'll talk about why
it's a good idea to shake up our beliefs from time to time.

One example is self-promotion. Many people have a phobia about
it, especially women, who are more likely to be self-critical than men.
(I run a very popular workshop called Shameless Self-Promotion.)
Our false belief is that humility is a sterling trait *under any and all
conditions*. That's ludicrous. No one searches for a tentative brain surgeon, a modest litigator, a self-disparaging consultant. People clearly
recognize that excellence requires pride (not arrogance) and comfort
in speaking about one's achievements. There's a belief that might be

stated as, "Good work should speak for itself." Maybe, but not usually. When credit is due, if you don't claim it, someone else will. All outstanding consultants know that the sequence for assigning credit can easily look like this:

1. Joan was instrumental in improving profitability.
2. Joan was of significant help.
3. Joan was highly supportive.
4. I don't think we needed Joan to do this.
5. Who's Joan?

This isn't a question of bragging or selfishness, but one of recognizing what you've accomplished.

Case Study

A consultant to a small law firm's managing partners told me he felt like a fraud because he himself had never managed a small law firm, though he was an attorney.

Upon questioning in front of 30 people, I established that: He had written more books on small law firm management than anyone in history; was cited in law newsletters for his expertise; had consulted with scores of such firms and had glowing testimonials; was interviewed by the media about the field; and was offered contracts by various legal outlets to use his intellectual property.

I told him there was no one alive more qualified than he was to consult with such clients. He had just refused to review his own incorrect belief system that you had to have done something to be able to give advice about it.

It seems to me that most of the life coaches we come across often do great work and help their clients substantially with issues that have been previously unresolvable. Yet most of these coaches don't make all that much money. They dislike self-promotion and depend on unsolicited referrals and people finding them. These talented coaches should learn to get recognized for the value they add.

I (Marshall) often explain it this way: If you came across a terrific product—say, a great car, an amazing TV series, or a sponge that never smelled like mildew—wouldn't you tell people about it? We've all found great products and evangelized about their merits to anyone who would listen. Because we didn't make them, we never feel self-conscious singing their praises. Now imagine you are the maker of those great products. You'd absolutely put the word out about how wonderful they are—while at the same time being accurate and avoiding any ridiculous hyperbole. The same goes for anything we're genuinely good at. If you tell people about it, you are giving them helpful information. There's no reason to be shy about that.

> **Milepost**
>
> You can't help others fully unless you're helping yourself first, which is why airlines tell you to put the oxygen mask on first before attempting to help others.

Let's create some definitions:

Confidence: The honest-to-God belief that you can help other people while also learning yourself.
Arrogance: The honest-to-God belief that you can help other people but have nothing left to learn yourself.
Smugness: Arrogance without the talent.
Brand: How someone thinks about you when you're not around. (Without a brand, they're not thinking of you!)

Here is what is *really* egotistical, however: The belief that one's work is *so outstanding that there is no need to promote it!* When you think of that belief not as humility but as a ridiculous expectation, you realize that it takes a lot of ego. That's a belief that is ingrained and unexamined. It's doubtful many people overtly say, "I'm so good that I can expect to just sit by the phone." Yet that's the unarticulated operating belief for many. Even the people with the strongest brands around don't make that arrogant assumption and continue to promote themselves.

A belief in positive self-promotion can actually be helpful in professional settings—when it prompts us to realize that we are always selling our ideas. Not only that, it is our responsibility to sell them, not others' responsibility to buy. I (Marshall) often share an idea that comes from the great management thinker Peter Drucker: Every decision is made by the person who has the power to make the decision—not necessarily the smartest person, or the one who is right. Once we make peace with that, and begin to focus on making a positive difference, we begin to have real influence. As Drucker said, "The great majority of people tend to focus downward. They are occupied with efforts rather than results. They worry over what the organization and their superiors 'owe' them and should do for them. And they are conscious above all of the authority they 'should have.' As a result they render themselves ineffectual."[1]

All companies have marketing functions. They believe in constant promotion. Fortunes are spent on advertising, product placement, and promotion. That's because it makes sense to place value on your product or service and not allow it to become a mere commodity that is compared simply on price, as if your clients were buying potatoes or paint.

Your work is no different. If you truly believe in the contribution that you can make, don't be ashamed to be your own marketing function!

We talked earlier about the imposter syndrome, wherein one is afraid of being "caught" because someone, somewhere—some omnipotence—has uncovered your weaknesses and lack of the

---

[1] Marshall Goldsmith, "How to Influence Decision Makers," *Harvard Business Review*, November 5, 2007, https://hbr.org/2007/11/how-to-influence-decision-make.

right to expound on your subject matter. When I began speaking professionally—for \$750 in the 1980s—I (Alan) was astounded that the audience was involved and invested in my plain common sense. I had no intricate models, no breakthrough visuals. But no one ever came up and dragged me off the stage. In fact, clients kept rehiring me, sometimes to deliver the exact same speech to the exact same people!

That was enlightening, and challenged my unspoken and heretofore unexamined belief that I needed new ideas and new forms of presentation to interest people. Instead, I was telling them pragmatically that if it hurt to do something, they should find a better way of doing it. I do the exact same thing today, but for a lot more money.

Case Study

A CEO who loved my talk in 1990 at his conference told me that he was impressed that I could be so creative so frequently. "After all," he said, "this presentation must have a shelf life of only about six months in these changing times."

"Right, thank you," I replied.

I'm still using the key points in that speech today (the difference between problem solving and innovation).

We often engage in behavior for no other reason than that we've never examined alternatives. Therefore we are subject to the inappropriate—and often damaging—attitudes and behaviors they generate. Some examples:

- We all need to be loved and approved of by everyone else.
- All problems have a clear solution.
- We have a duty to intervene when others are unhappy.
- Every grievance has a right to be aired and corrected.
- We should sacrifice for others, especially family.
- We have no control over "them."

- We can't influence tomorrow.
- It is right to dwell and ruminate on fearful possibilities.
- It is better to tolerate dysfunctional behavior than to confront it.

These beliefs alter our behaviors and cause *us* to be dysfunctional.

Challenging and Evaluating Your Belief System

One important aspect of examining our beliefs is understanding our *identities*. We often perceive our "real" selves as inferior to the people others see and with whom they interact. We think we have to play a role to gain social acceptance. The existentialist philosopher Jean Paul Sartre dealt with this concept through his famous example of "the waiter." He describes a waiter who is "overly a waiter," too polite, too well put together, too knowledgeable. (We've all had an overly solicitous waiter who seems too eager to serve, frequently checking on our gustatory progress and actually interrupting our dinner.) Sartre argues that social pressure has prompted the waiter to act out values he doesn't really have. In the process, the waiter loses a piece of his conscious freedom. Sartre claims that most people don't even recognize that they are giving this freedom away.

In our eagerness to succeed—perhaps the most intense type of social pressure in American society—it is easy to lose that freedom. Instead of living our real values, we adopt the values we think we're supposed to have. When we hear that charismatic people are successful, we try to seem charismatic (even if that's an awkward fit for our personality). Some of us try to hang onto our authenticity by describing ourselves how we *want* to be seen.

Once again, let's consider the plight of the waiter—though not Sartre's waiter this time. Earlier, we talked about Los Angeles waiters with aspirations to be on television. They might boldly describe themselves as actors, even though they haven't played any parts yet. A dentist might describe herself as a screenwriter, though she has only a few pages completed. The consultant describes himself as a sought-after speaker and world-class authority when in reality he has just a few clients.

There's no harm in a little positive self-deception (which research has shown can actually be good for you in small doses). But too much of it sends our lives off track. That's because it's difficult to be authentic if we identify with someone we haven't become and who is actually not visible to others. I don't see an aspiring actor, I see and interact with a waiter. I don't see a hopeful screenwriter, I see my dentist. A great many people have told me that they're novelists, yet they've never published a book commercially and they're editing the writing of others or working as an underwriter.

Your belief system needs to be adjusted to what is, so that you can make decisions and take actions in the present that reflect the real you and what you're actually doing—authentically. Otherwise, the waiter doesn't focus on igniting his acting career because in his own mind he is already an actor. The dentist is so focused on her screenplay that she overlooks some shadows on an X-ray. The consultant spends more time touting his meager successes than building new business.

In coaching, we meet people daily who struggle in their roles because they identify with a role others can't see. It can even be tough being a parent if you see yourself as a public relations professional or a real estate agent, one for whom taking care of a child is "temporary" until a nanny or day care is possible. It's extremely difficult for many people to see themselves as retired when they are fit, sharp, energetic, and see themselves as executives, truckers, or pilots.

One of the most fascinating debates in the airline industry concerns the long-standing requirement that pilots retire at 65. Both of us are over this age and are at the height of our powers and our ability to help others, and are more successful than when we were young. Why should an otherwise fit man or woman be denied a job because of an arbitrary age limit? In fact, we can easily make the case (as have many pilots) that it is an absurd business decision to remove your most highly experienced, successful people for no other reason than an age chosen from antiquity. (Moreover, they are the best trainers of others.)

The Social Security Act was passed in the United States in 1935, when 65 was considered old age and the average lifespan was about 68. It was expected that someone retiring and collecting social security would do so for about three years, supported by contributions made by about a dozen workers—12 people working for every retired person, a dozen people contributing to a system for every one person withdrawing from it.

Today, 65 is the new 50, the average life span is 78, and to apply the same math you would have people withdrawing from the system for *13 years on average*, with about only two people contributing on the job. Those pilots could easily take yearly physicals and work for another five years or more—highly qualified professionals who continue to contribute. George Bernard Shaw observed that "Men don't stop playing games because they grow old, men grow old because they stop playing games."

If we return to external control and allow our environment and "wise men" to tell us that we should expect to slow down, deteriorate, and decline at an arbitrary age, we create a self-fulfilling prophecy of despair. We do see a great many people who, removed from the rigors and demands of their lifelong passions, decline rapidly. Planting a garden doesn't replace debating legal issues. Helping your grandchildren to ride a bike is not mutually exclusive with building homes. Too many people who scrimp and save for retirement see their nest eggs gobbled up by health needs when they finally retire and the sedentary results creates unexpected illness, mental and physical.

I (Marshall) have also seen misguided beliefs about retirement set people's lives on the wrong track. My friend Dave retired at 48, after his company was acquired. He was worth millions and no longer needed to work. He had time, resources, and energy to do whatever he wanted. He planned a life of travel, golf, and time with his wife and family. Life was going to be wonderful.

Six months later, Dave was home—alone and miserable. The kids were away at college. After the remodeling of their home, his wife had become bored. She poured herself into a new job and seemed to be gone a good deal of the time.

One day, a deliveryman came over to drop off a package. Dave's house was his last stop for the day, so Dave asked him in. Over a cup of coffee, the two engaged in what became a fascinating discussion. The courier surprised Dave with his keen insight into current global problems and his grasp of complex economic issues. "What a neat conversation," Dave later thought. "In fact, that conversation was so much fun, it was the highlight of my week!"

It was a revelation. When Dave looked in the mirror that afternoon, he saw the face of a guy who had been watching reruns of *Everybody Loves Raymond* on TV. For fun, he was playing mediocre golf and listening to old men at the country club repeat the same old war stories about what they used to do. He asked himself, "Did I just say the highlight of my week was talking with the delivery guy about the world's problems?"

Within two weeks, Dave had a new job. He realized that retirement, or even thinking and planning for retirement, wasn't all that it was supposed to be.

I (Marshall) have had the privilege of getting to know many of the top thinkers in my field. They could all retire if they wanted to. But most do not. People like Peter Drucker, former Girl Scouts leader Frances Hesselbein, and Warren Bennis have struck me as amazing. They just kept on making great contributions. They didn't keep working for money, prestige, or status. They kept working because they loved their work, and they were making a positive difference in the world. Together with my friend Dave, they have taught me a great lesson: Our traditional notion of retirement is greatly overrated.

I was lucky enough to be with one of the most respected consultants in organizational change, Richard Beckhard, a couple of days before he died. Dick was a great coach and mentor to me, as well as an inspiration for many people in our field. When I last visited him, Dick knew that his life was almost over. His doctor respected him enough to let him know that he was not going to recover, and he needed to say his last farewells.

As I watched Dick answer a series of phone calls, I found him not only saying good-bye. He was continuing to help other people. I was amazed at the excitement and enthusiasm he was able to convey. He was working with people in the same caring and effective way he always had.

My first thought was, "Dick, why don't you just let it go and take care of yourself? You've done enough." Fortunately, I kept my mouth shut. Dick was still smiling, still able to laugh, still filled with passion. He knew that he wasn't going to be around to collect the consulting fees for his final assignments. It didn't really matter. He was still doing a great job—even from his deathbed. In that instant, I made a decision. I decided that I wanted to be like Dick Beckhard when I grew up.

I like recalling that moment, because it's a relatively rare example of when one of my beliefs changed. People often change their beliefs about critical issues if they're willing to listen to opposing views, even on controversial topics (yes, it can happen, even though it's far too rare in our political discourse). Many have obviously changed their beliefs about drinking while driving, or cigarettes, or what does and does not constitute a medical disorder.

Here's a quick test to challenge and evaluate your beliefs:

1. What are your basic beliefs about yourself; e.g., what you are great at (teaching), what you just can't do (play an instrument), how you respond (impatient), and so forth?
2. What merits reconsideration and/or change (you could take piano lessons, learn to swim better, leave your corporate job and start your own business)?
3. What actions and behaviors should be modified, created, abandoned, in light of those changes (resign from a group, confront a poor relationship, make different investments)?

You probably don't do this too often, if at all. Yet without a conscious evaluation of our beliefs, they can become sclerotic. We assume they're true and shouldn't change. We act, therefore, as if they are continually valid in determining our lives. But none of us is the person we were a year ago, let alone five years ago, or whenever these beliefs were inscribed in our cerebellum. In fact, one of my lines that draws the greatest acknowledgements in audiences is, "I'm constantly surprised by how stupid I was two weeks ago."

Maybe it's time to change our attitudes.

The Creation of Attitudes for Growth

Attitudes are the connectors—the synapses—between beliefs and behavior, a self-comforting way of thinking or feeling about someone or something, typically reflected in a person's behavior. Thus, people who have never, ever tasted uni (sea urchin, a Japanese delicacy) will tell you they can't stand it, because their attitude is that the consistency and look are foreboding. Attitudes can be paradoxical (Yogi Berra's famous observation that "No one ever goes there anymore, it's too crowded"), can be lifelong (I feel uncomfortable in or near the water), can be widely shared (I feel lazy if I'm not working on something), and can vary tremendously culturally (the Japanese rarely inform a family member that the person has cancer, with even the doctor participating in the disinformation and deception). The Germans and Australians (admittedly generalizing here) generally don't react well to indications of wealth among people they consider peers, while Americans admire it and want to find out how to accomplish it.

In business (and in schools) attitudes are often unjustifiably and wrongly attributed. Someone late for a meeting "isn't a team player," although in truth she or he might have been delayed by a personal issue or a traffic jam. A student is often described as having a bad attitude when the culprit is really dyslexia, confusing material, or poor teaching. Bob Mager famously observed that if some one can't perform after you put a gun to his head, he has a knowledge or skills problem. If that person suddenly *can* perform after you put a gun to his head, he has an attitude or motivation problem.[2]

You can train someone—build the skills—when there are performance deficits, but you have to coach people with dysfunctional

---

[2]Robert F. Mager and Peter Pipe, *Analyzing Performance Problems* (Belmont, CA: Lake Publishing, 1984).

attitude issues, which is why blanket motivational, educational, and operational programs rarely work in the business world.

Case Study

In 2016 Wells Fargo underwent a well-documented investigation by authorities after it was determined that thousands of employees had opened and traded in fraudulent accounts to gain commissions for themselves and meet quotas, at the expense of customers. Senior management denied knowledge of a hugely widespread practice. Executives were equated to bank robbers by members of Congress during the hearings.

The belief system at the bank was that if you met your quotas you were protected and golden. If you didn't, you were out the door. All of the cues in the environment supported those beliefs. The ensuing attitude in thousands of diverse employees was, therefore, "I need to follow those practices, which everyone is doing without consequence, not only to make money and advance, but even to merely keep my job."

The resulting behavior was, of course, criminal. But that's how easy it is to cross ethical and legal boundaries when you have the wrong attitudes.

So what of your attitudes? If you change your beliefs, your attitudes should commensurately change, and your behaviors should follow suit:

- If you now believe that it's unethical to eat animals, then your attitude becomes one of refusing meat and your behavior becomes vegetarian.
- If you now believe that smoking is bad for you and your family, your attitude may be to dissuade your children from smoking and resist smoking environments, and your behavior might

include changing your wardrobe to remove the clothing that smells of tobacco.

- If you now believe that you are helping people in offering value, and not merely trying to sell them something to make money, your attitude might now be that you need to reach out more and your behavior becomes one of asking for referrals and making proactive phone calls.

Attitudes for our own growth would include statements and observations such as these:

- I need to acquire my own developmental resources.
- There's nothing wrong with failure if I learn from it.
- I can take prudent risk without serious threat to the family.
- I must accept the inconvenience of travel away from home.
- I need to be honest and vulnerable to be coached properly.

Attitudes are often most seriously influenced by peers. This places a high premium on who you hang out with. On your evolutionary journey, it's wise to consider the clubs, associations, and institutions to which you belong. What do you read? To what do you subscribe? Who are your friends? Where do you spend most of your social time? What boards or committees are you on? What are your local political connections? To what causes do you contribute?

We talked earlier about sealing the watertight doors on the past so that you can move forward with the next stages of your life. Inertia— the tendency of a body not in motion to remain not in motion— can create a super glue that keeps you "stuck" with conditions that represent outmoded and irrelevant attitudes.

Logic makes us think, but emotions make us act.

The objective, periodic review of our attitudes is vital because they are the director of how we act, the behaviors that manifest our belief system. Therefore, it's best to focus on the wisdom of our intentions before we actually demonstrate them.

Beliefs Manifest in Behavior

What if we told you that you can create your own reality? Life is a bit like a new, sophisticated video game in which your wraparound goggles can be programmed to reflect the reality of your choosing. Wouldn't that be diverting, and even all consuming? Wouldn't the lines between the game and reality begin to blur?

We are all playing that game, and we are all (figuratively) wearing those wraparound goggles, all the time. That's why, if we care about accuracy, and about being conscious of the reality we occupy, we should periodically question our deepest assumptions.

There was a 1956 science fiction movie from MGM called *Forbidden Planet* that ushered in the color and cinemascope era. It's considered a classic, almost Shakespearean in motif, and introduced a quite impressive Robby the Robot. The actors were all well known and the effects quite startling. The "monsters" in the film turned out to be the products of the protagonist's (Mobius's) own imagination, brought to life by his computers.

Mobius created his own reality just as we, too, can create our own reality and our own monsters. Our behaviors are influenced by this constructed reality, which is then, reciprocally, influenced by our behaviors.

Accurate Thinking & Assumptions & Appearances

How is this possible?

We behave consistently with our beliefs and attitudes, and those beliefs and attitudes can be heavily laden with assumptions. Individuals and organizations can make poor decisions based on invalid assumptions.

Have you ever assumed that your car is full of gas when it is, in fact, empty? Or that:

- You would receive the next promotion available?
- You were receiving an A in a critical course?
- Your partner agrees with your vacation choice?
- Your kids would never do drugs or drink alcohol?
- Your client was happy with the project?

- Your chronic pain was nothing serious?
- You could drive no matter what the road conditions?

And have those assumptions ever proved false, causing pain, inconvenience, rifts in relationships, accidents, and trauma?

We think we're seeing and immersed in universal truths, but we're actually engaged in our own reality (perceptions _are_ reality, because we act based upon them). What we see, and the assumptions _Mirage_ we make based on that sight, is overwhelmingly compelling, far more than information received from other senses. Yet the accuracy is often suspect, giving a perverse and different meaning to the comic line, "Who do you believe, me or your lying eyes?"

It's easy to be caught up in the lure of false assumptions. Sometimes we misinterpret what appear to be clear facts. Law officers and prosecutors will tell you that eyewitness testimony is not all that reliable.[3] We talked earlier about how we feel we can order more food when the server is overweight, or how we feel better about our weight when we hang out with heavier people. Similarly, after we exercise rigorously and we look at a hill, the hill appears to be steeper than if we were asked about it before exercising. We're looking at the same hill in nature, but with what is often called a different set of eyes. After a recent train crash caused by high speed, New Jersey Transit required the conductor join the engineer in the cab when nearing two of its stations, to provide another set of eyes at a critical juncture.

How we feel and what we experience impacts what we "see" and what we see impacts how we feel and what we experience, which is a dynamic rife with assumptions. That's what we mean by creating our own reality. I've attended a speech that was brilliant and captivating, and afterward learned that the speaker was distraught about the performance, believing that it was subpar. I'm always amazed by pedestrians who dart out in front of moving cars, not the least bit concerned that speeding cars will hit them.

---

[3] In a classic law school experiment, a person rushes into a first-year course in front of 100 students, grabs a book, and runs out another door. The students' descriptions of the intruder vary tremendously when later interviewed.

Who's right?

Here are some issues to consider when facing the inevitable opportunity to create your own reality:

Fear distorts your reality. When we fear what is approaching, we tend to withdraw, procrastinate, and deny. Our assumption is that almost anything is better than ambiguity and uncertainty. This is why some of the best leaders we've ever seen are those who are comfortable working in ambiguous circumstances, and who do not try to avoid them.

Uncertainty undermines critical thought processes. Instead of finding causes of problems, or creating outcomes for decisions, we take refuge in inaction. This means we take a back seat to the people who know how to be swift and decisive.

Confrontation is an important life skill. If we don't confront fear, attempt to validate assumptions, and verify what we see, *our lives will be determined by others and by our false assumptions*. Confrontation does not have to be hostile. It's merely the act of sorting the true from the false, the real from the unreal.

Our *internal naysayer must be silenced once and for all*. The hesitancy to speak, or write, or act results in behaviors that are passive and unimpressive. More importantly, we surrender control.

Internal Naysayer

Milepost

The only thing worse than being blind is having sight but no vision.

—Helen Keller

Beliefs form attitudes that are manifest in behavior. We've spoken about deliberately and consciously examining and changing both beliefs and attitudes, and now we're suggesting that you investigate the assumptions you're making about the world around you—the world you're creating—and not simply believe what you're told.

No Swimming With 1 Hour

Observations can also be used to dispel assumptions. At one point we were told very seriously by experts that we shouldn't swim within an hour of eating a meal. I recall us on the beach carefully watching the time—surely 55 minutes might still be dangerous—until we could return to the ocean after our ham sandwiches. (Having learned to scuba dive, I adhered to the same time regimens in terms of nitrogen building in the blood, and always wondered about the "science" behind that, too!) Yet we never observed scores of people who eschewed this advice cramping and drowning. Similarly, it used to be an article of faith that we lose more heat from our heads than from other parts of our bodies—which is why generations of parents insisted kids wear hats. In fact, heat escapes from our heads no faster than from the rest of us.[4]

We have to match our sensory intake (which is mainly visual) with our intellectual processing, making sure that we don't undermine the latter with false interpretations of the former. My German shepherd has 6 million more olfactory detectors than I do, and my beagle has 6 million more than he does! Their sense of smell is much more accurate than ours! And yet, as far as anyone knows, they don't make assumptions.

When we constantly question our beliefs, rethink our attitudes, and evaluate our behavior, we stay awake and aware on our journey through life.

---

[4] Ian Sample, "Scientists Debunk the Myth That You Lose Most Heat through Your Head," *Guardian*, December 17, 2008, https://www.theguardian.com/science/2008/dec/17/medicalresearch-humanbehaviour.

5 | The Importance and Evolution of Character

Character's Composition

When we talk about the singer Bono, we tend to introduce him with the descriptor "the rock star," or we place the appositive thereafter. So it's:

The rock star, Bono...
Bono, the rock star...

It's inevitable that we end up defining people by their best-known traits, as with swimmer Michael Phelps or Lady Gaga, the performer. But too much emphasis on a title can create the mistaken impression that a person's real identity is singular and stable. In fact, we are constantly changing and growing.

A few years ago, I (Marshall) had the opportunity to sit next to Bono at a charity fundraiser. I was 66 years old at the time, and since his music was recorded some time after 1975, I'd never heard of it. Fortunately for me, he did not discuss his music. He discussed his life.

After listening to Bono share his personal story, I realized that he is a wonderful example of a person who has not only changed his behavior but also his identity, or definition of who he is—while remaining authentic and not becoming a phony. Bono's early identity was "regular guy." He was not brought up rich and had a disdain for pretension. It was easy to see how he has maintained this identity.

In our one-on-one conversation, as well as in his after-dinner speech, Bono was self-deprecating. As we spoke, his language was very much regular guy. He politely apologized to me for using variations of the f-word a few times. (I assured him that this language was not troubling to me. As a teenager I thought it was the adjective that preceded most nouns.)

After "regular guy" he became a "rock 'n' roll fan." He was animated in his discussion of the musicians who had influenced this life—and how much he enjoyed listening to them as a youth. In his speech he was generous in his praise for other musicians and in his admiration of their work.

Bono's next identity was "musician." He described how he had made a commitment to his craft—and how much he enjoyed what he did. He talked about the joy of playing with friends when no status or money was involved. The identity after that—the one most of us know—was "rock star." He clearly liked being a rock star and enjoyed the fame.

As much as he remained a regular guy, was clearly a huge rock 'n' roll fan, loved being a musician, and enjoyed the life of a rock star—Bono was even more excited about his new role: humanitarian. He recounted his experience of visiting Africa during the great famine of the 1980s. (I spent time there as a Red Cross volunteer, and I could relate to this experience.) He talked about his desire to help those who needed help the most and to alleviate human suffering. It was clear that a large part of the rest of his life would be devoted to doing whatever he could to make our world a better place.

In his after-dinner speech he did not take cheap shots at politicians, governments, or anyone else—even when certain questions teed up this opportunity. He was clearly there to raise money and to help people in need—not to prove how smart or clever he was. He was sincere in expressing gratitude to anyone who was helping out in any way. His need to help others far exceeded his need to be right. He is a man with a mission. He isn't pretending to be a humanitarian—he is a humanitarian. He did not let his definition of who he was limit his potential for who he could become.[1]

Case Study

I (Alan) remember seeing a backpack all alone on a seat at an airport departure gate. I observed that after 20 minutes of my noticing it, no one had come for it. My first thought was that someone would surely inform security, or that the security people would notice themselves. After all, I was just a consultant changing planes and probably overreacting. What did I know about security?

I realized a thousand people were passing by this backpack and I finally got up and found a police officer. He thanked me and went over to investigate. My attitude was wrong. What if everyone simply said, "That's not who I am" and never bothered with anything else?

The point is, *a shift in your identity doesn't make you a phony*. You are allowed to fill new roles and take on new responsibilities. You may hang back, wondering "Who am I to . . ."

- Tell a teacher that there is too much homework?
- Ask for a meal not on the menu?
- Address this particular group on that topic?
- Offer to be chair of the fundraising committee?
- Lobby the town counsel for a stop sign at a dangerous corner?

---

[1] Marshall Goldsmith, *MOJO: How to Get It, How to Keep It, How to Get It Back If You Lose It* (New York: Hyperion, 2009).

We encourage you be willing to take on new roles. Where once our commentary or intervention was improper, now it may be precisely relevant. (Or it may have never been improper at all.) Most of us truly appreciate how best to change something after we experience it, and our input is most valued after we've done it. That's why hotels and airlines send us questionnaires about the service after the stay and after the flight.

Character evolves. Your circumstances change. Robespierre claimed that, "No man can step outside the shadow of his own character." But the shadow changes because of our growth and the angle of the light.

Here are six elements of what we've come to call character:

1. *Intelligence:* The ability to apply critical thinking skills to problems and challenges. Separating how one thinks about something from what one feels about it. Aptitude for learning. The ability to quickly discern and apply patterns and identify distinctions.

2. *Drive or assertiveness:* The ability to identify the need for and to create urgency. A goal orientation. Moving through and around obstacles that block others. Finding ways to make something happen rather than creating excuses about why something can't happen.

3. *Happiness:* As characterized in Dan Gilbert's work[2] at Harvard, happiness isn't merely about the fortunate circumstances life brings us by chance, but our ability to create "synthetic" happiness (which we often dismiss negatively as rationalization). My getting fired *was* one of the best things that ever happened to me, just as a broken arm, a car crash, or a missed flight may be one of yours. Seeking and achieving well-being on our own terms is an essential aspect of character.

4. *Empathy:* Part of strong character and a virtuous life is the ability to put yourself in others' shoes and understand how they feel. The extension of kindness and the genuine regard for others

---

[2] Daniel Gilbert, *Stumbling on Happiness* (New York: Knopf, 2007).

is a wonderful character trait. This is why passive-aggressive behavior ("You daughter was accepted at Michigan? Congratulations. I assume that was her back-up school?") reflects weak character, because it is malicious and seeks to subtly undermine others.

5. *Reciprocity and friendship:* The ability to give as well as take, to contribute as much as benefit, is a strong element of character. Introversion is not a negative, but the unwillingness to help others and to create friendships is. Healthy people maintain friendships, although as we discussed earlier, some of these may and should change with our circumstances. Character is never static, and neither are our relationships.

6. *Intimacy and trust:* Strong character demands the ability to form loving bonds and to allow for vulnerability. The people we coach who make the most progress the fastest are those who are comfortable exposing their fears and weaknesses—being vulnerable in front of others. People incapable of creating strong, intimate bonds in their lives are affected by a key character flaw.

Character Test

Rate yourself on a 1-to-5 scale on our six elements:

1. Can't really say that this is at all like me.
2. Occasionally, I could be described this way.
3. In some circumstances, I'm always like this.
4. This usually describes me.
5. I'm constantly like this.

	Score
Intelligence	_____
Drive	_____
Happiness	_____
Empathy	_____
Reciprocity	_____
Intimacy	_____

We're not asking you to total these elements because the point is to raise each of them to the maximum level. There is no total score above which you are fine if any of the individual ones are low. Our feeling is that a 4 or 5 is needed in each element. Which, if any, are your weak points?

To build character, you need to build these six elements. To evolve character, you need to evolve these elements. Our recommendations:

1. *Intelligence:* Read widely and diversely, including fiction, history, biography, science, and philosophy. Don't allow social media to be your news source. Read the *New York Times*, *Wall Street Journal*, and similar publications daily. Try to solve word and math problems. Practice writing your opinions in a blog or newsletter, then move to letters to the editor and op-ed pieces. Attend discussion groups, participate in mastermind groups, and invest in self-development experiences. The finest return you'll ever obtain derives from an investment in yourself.

2. *Drive:* Create short-term deadlines. Identify two priorities a day (personal and/or professional) that *must* be completed. Use a calendar to record your metrics for progress by predetermined dates. Don't look for blame; find the causes of obstacles and then work to remove them. Don't rely on others or wait for others, take control of your route to your goals.

3. *Happiness:* Find the silver lining in any circumstance. Convince yourself that failing is a learning experience and that failing is far better than never trying. Make the best of situations. If your travel connection is missed, use the time to call friends or prospects, or to write a proposal you've been meaning to get to. Buy a book you wouldn't otherwise have picked up. At the beginning of the day remind yourself of why you're going to make it a great one, and at the end of the day review what went well, no matter how minor. Focus on the improvements in your behavior (your character) and not on achieving victories that are defined by someone else's criteria.

4. *Empathy:* Think about similar circumstances you've experienced as you listen to someone else. Try not to make judgments, but to listen and understand. Don't position yourself as a teacher but rather as a colleague. Ask for more details, even if you believe you've understood the circumstances. Encourage the other person to talk.

5. *Reciprocity:* Identify how you would like to be treated if you were the other person (not necessarily as you've been treated in the past). Don't hesitate to give more than you received. Don't expect a thank you for something that you're doing as a courtesy or to help. (A lot of us allow a car to cross in front of us in heavy traffic, but some of us become incensed when the other driver doesn't offer a formal thanks!) Accept the fact that reciprocity doesn't have to be immediate in all cases.

6. *Intimacy:* Be willing to talk about "defeats" and setbacks. Call a failure a failure. Ask others you trust (trust, hence intimacy) what reactions and advice they have. Be open to hearing another's burning issues even if you consider them to be trivial or irrelevant. Proactively ask for help and opinions. Make an effort to stop being embarrassed by personal questions and expressions of personal feelings.

I (Marshall) agree wholeheartedly that these are great building blocks for character. To remind myself to practice these and other values, I have developed a system.

As I mentioned earlier, I pay a woman to call me up every day and ask me a series of questions: Did I do my best to be happy that day? Set goals? Make progress on those goals? Say or do something nice for my wife, my son, my daughter, and my grandchildren? I came up with these and some 40 other questions myself, a brief self-test on my life's main priorities. My caller offers no judgment, just listens politely and perhaps offers a few general words of encouragement before hanging up.

This process, which I call the Daily Questions, keeps me focused on becoming a happier, healthier person. It provides discipline I sorely need in my busy working life as an executive coach, teacher, and speaker, which involves traveling 180 days out of the year to countries all over the globe. I have been doing this system for years, and I recommend it to my coaching clients. As of this writing, some 5,000 people have taken an online version of the Daily Questions, and they have reported overwhelmingly that it helped them stay true to their values and priorities.

A disciplined approach such as the Daily Questions holds us accountable. Day after day, it requires us to face the same questions. Like water dripping on a rock, this gradual pressure can eventually wear away at the toughest, most intransigent problems. It is not always easy, but it is character forming in the literal sense of the term. We build who we are through our behavior, day in and day out. This is true no matter how successful we become. We can always develop more character. That's an important aspect of lifestorming.[3]

Ethical and Moral Behavior

When we talk about ethical behavior, we usually mean:

- Relating to moral principles or the branch of knowledge dealing with these principles
- Morally good or correct
- Avoiding activities or organizations that do harm to people or the environment

When we talk of moral behavior, it is usually:

- Concerned with the principles of right and wrong behavior and the goodness or badness of human character
- Concerned with or derived from the code of interpersonal behavior that is considered right or acceptable in a particular society
- Holding or manifesting high principles for proper conduct

---

[3] Marshall Goldsmith and Mark Reiter, *Triggers: Creating Behavior That Lasts—Becoming the Person You Want to Be* (New York: Crown Publishing, 2015).

Our society's views on ethics and morality have changed. Industries once freely dumped waste into rivers and lakes. Animals were hunted for the sake of killing and trophies, with extinction of the species of no concern—just a few examples of the remarkable shift in values over the past 50 to 70 years. Without asking you to dig out your notes from Philosophy 101, here are two of the schools of thought on ethics and morality:

Utilitarianism: A philosophy advocated by John Stuart Mill, Jeremy Bentham, and others, which called for the greatest good for the greatest number. An act is ethical if it benefits most people; never mind the adverse consequence for some.

Deontology: Deontology is the ethical position that an act is inherently right or wrong in itself, irrespective of who benefits. Kant created the categorical imperative, which basically asks, what if everyone did this? If the act is considered good but the consequence of everyone doing it is bad, then it's an unethical act. (In my professional life, I find myself constantly responding to requests for an exception of some kind with, "If I allowed you to do this I'd have to allow everyone to do it, and that would be untenable.")

These different approaches to morality and ethics demonstrate the conundrums often faced when trying to decide what the right thing to do actually is. In a famous movie called *Lifeboat* made in 1944 from a story by John Steinbeck, the survivors of a torpedoed ship can only survive if their overcrowded lifeboat is reduced in population. The boat's senior officer has to make agonizing efforts to save those he can while sacrificing others, but by what criteria does one do this?

And what has this to do with your journey?

We compete daily. Perhaps not as obviously as two fighters in an arena, but we compete against others (and ourselves) in terms of performance and accomplishment. We vie for space, whether on the highway or in an elevator. We seek airtime to have our cases heard at meetings. We seek to influence (see the following segment) prospects, superiors, and colleagues. We face crises in terms of trauma, abrupt changes in our routines, health, and relationships. We are stymied at times through no fault of our own, and often no fault of anyone else. Even championship games can be rained out.

This competition often forces tough choices on us, and those pressures can cause us to compromise our ideals, principles, and values. Those compromises can become ethical transgressions. Examples include the person desperate for a key job who lies about a college graduate degree and is exposed five years later when in a much more exalted position, or the person who spreads rumor and innuendo about a third party in order to gain favor with the instigator.

As I (Marshall) mentioned earlier, I don't advise organizations to coach their way out of ethics violations. People who make these mistakes should be fired. By tolerating ethics violations, companies send an "ethics is optional" message. When companies allow ethics violations to slide with a slap on the wrist or a corrective coaching session, the perpetrators don't grasp the seriousness of what they've done wrong.

Our advice follows what is usually attributed to Jefferson: "In matters of taste, swim with the current. In matters of principle, stand like a rock." The importance of character is paramount in your journey, and the embrace of ethical conduct and behavior is the foundation of character.

A Slow, Steady March

The evolutionary journey is not grandiose, but gradual. It's about doing something—even small things—every day, not waiting for huge leaps and otherwise doing nothing. Children evolve very quickly. Why should we be different as adults? But in adults, evolution must be intentional. If we don't deliberately pursue our evolution it won't happen.

Look around at friends, colleagues, and acquaintances. How many have feathered a nest and have virtually stopped their lives and growth? How many actually advocate *against* change and instead prefer that they (and you) settle for comfort? Yet, as we discussed in the last chapter, both of us are circling 70 and are still evolving. Shaquille O'Neal, the former basketball All-Star, has a PhD, is worth about $300 million, and is having a great time with his life. Michael Strahan was an All-Star football lineman, and is now a highly acclaimed morning talk show host. Jimmy Carter left the presidency and became a respected international monitor of free elections and supporter of human rights around the globe.

We hope that, like us, you have friends, family, and colleagues who are constantly evolving. When my (Alan's) grandmother was hospitalized briefly, the doctor told us she was doing quite well for a 79-year-old. We asked her why she had lied about her actual age, which was 85. "Because," she told us, "after you're 80 they don't care any more." (She was somewhere between 101 and 104 when she passed away!)

When I was working at the dean of students office at Rutgers in my senior year, the dean stopped by and asked how I was doing in my final year. I told him I felt great, that I had a sense of command that I never had had before.

"That's the power of learning," he observed, "nothing else like it."

Learning is power. Those of us engaged in lifelong learning—whether seven or seventy—are constantly enhancing our power. Our evolutionary journey is one of accumulating power so that we can help ourselves and others.

Case Study

I was doing a pro bono speech for the Phoenix chapter of the National Speakers Association. It was summer, 114 degrees in the shade, so the chapter began the meeting at 8 A.M. before the real heat set in. I was picked up at my hotel at 7 and arrived at 7:30, tired and somewhat ornery.

I grabbed some coffee and walked into the meeting room to familiarize myself with the setup. To my surprise, a man and woman were already seated in the front row. As I approached, my surprise turned to shock, because the man was the legendary Cavett Robert, who founded the National Speakers Association, was internationally acclaimed, and was around 90 years of age. His daughter, Lee, was with him. I knew both of them.

"What on earth are you doing here?!" I said, before I could think better of it. Lee thought that I meant what were they doing in the front row, and tried to explain that her father was hard of hearing. But he knew exactly what I meant and said, "I'm here to learn something. You'd better be good!"

As I recall, I rose to the occasion—which is a good thing, considering that the illustrious Cavett Robert woke up at 6:30 in the morning to drive in from the outskirts of town to hear me speak! At age 90, he was still active and engaged in learning—which shows me that anyone can do it if they have the volition.

We have to be lifelong learners and continually gain power over:

- *Health:* What do we need to do to sustain good health, especially as our physical condition changes? What can we be proactive about and what should we be reactive about? What are only fads and myths and what is fact? What kind of physical activity is best for us?
- *Money:* How much will we need at different points in our life for what kind of lifestyle? How should investment strategies change? How much risk tolerance do I have and should I have? What kind of banking relationships should I create?
- *Relationships:* Are there long-term, poor relationships that ought to be repaired (or abandoned)? Are you developing new and appropriate relationships for your career? Are you making the most of relationships to expand your horizons, gain work, and grow?
- *Happiness:* Are you enlarging your sources of happiness? Can you synthesize happiness by making lemonade from lemons and

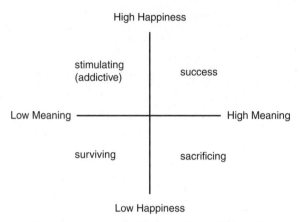

Figure 5.1 Happiness and Meaning

a citrus industry from lemonade? Are you creating happiness for others and sharing yours with friends and family?

- *Meaning:* Happiness and meaning are interrelated. Too many of us believe that we are engaged in a search for meaning. The truth is that we should be oriented toward *creating* meaning. The creation of meaning involves the perpetuation of our own happiness.

  Lifestorming is about the independent and bold creation of meaning for ourselves, shunning the external meaning often foist upon us by society and the media. Figure 5.1 reflects this relationship.

In the bottom left of Figure 5.1, people are merely surviving. They are unhappy and see no meaning in life. This is true alienation and may even be self-destructive. People in this sector have nothing to live for and no will to create anything to live for.

In the lower right of the figure we have sacrificing. Meaning is high but happiness is low, so we throw ourselves into the work or the cause or the direction. We sacrifice our time and our own objectives because there is nothing that we perceive worth fighting for or preserving. We see people in this sector putting in very long hours at the office or completely consumed by their volunteer work. (And sometimes we see them prolonging bad marriages and lousy relationships.)

The top left is the stimulating position. We might refer to this as "addictive." This is the sector where people have huge happiness that is devoid of meaning. Those who abuse drugs and/or alcohol are in this sector. You probably know people who work out obsessively, beyond their actual needs. Also here are those with eating disorders and those who are workaholics. Addictive behavior needn't be obvious, but it's detrimental all the same.

Finally, we have the successes in the upper right of the figure. They are happy and lead lives full of meaning (they are happy *because* they lead lives full of meaning). There is meaning in their lives and they are happy (there is meaning in their lives *because* they are happy). They realize the reciprocity between happiness and meaning.

Our position is that just as no one should consume wealth without creating wealth, no one should consume happiness without creating happiness. There should be no one who is simply a taker and consumer.

We need meaning and happiness to lead great lives. This is the essence of lifestorming—we have to find qualities ourselves.

The Meaning of Presence

The word "presence" has gained new currency among leadership thinkers in recent years. I might quibble with the term (somehow "charisma" has more, well, charisma than presence), but not with the notion behind it: That those who have it are *immediately* effective, highly regarded, and heeded. Who hasn't wished to be that person who:

- Is never interrupted when speaking.
- Causes a hush in the room.
- Makes an endorsement that is immediately effective.
- Has people clamoring to be part of the team.
- Admits to an error with no repercussions.

- Always receives the benefit of the doubt.
- Can propel a new idea forward, or derail it.
- Is sought out as a teammate and a dinner companion.

We've found that people can gain presence during the evolutionary journey. It isn't so much a learned skill as it is the accumulation and resultant synergy of experiences, new learning, fearlessness, and high esteem (confidence). Sometimes you may possess it and not even realize it.

Case Study

I was working with a leading IT company where it was common to find myself in large meetings. As often happens in big gatherings of smart people, discussions tended to bounce around the room like a ball in a pinball machine, without necessarily closing in on the goal.

After 30 minutes of debate at one meeting, there was a lull. I hadn't said a thing up to this point, so I ambled up to the flip chart, drew a visual of where we were and where we ought to be, then listed three alternatives for successfully making the move. I suggested we all look at benefits and risk and choose the most desirable alternative. We did so. I did the same thing in the next meeting a couple of weeks later.

To me this was nothing all that special. As a consultant, I was just doing my job. But my key contact told me that these few interactions had impressed the clients so much that I was now considered "the primary change agent expert for the company." I never thought of myself as a person with presence, but apparently my years of experience had instilled this quality in me without my even knowing it. If I can develop presence mostly by accident in the normal course of my daily work, you can certainly do it with conscious intention.

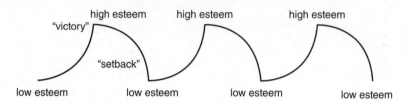

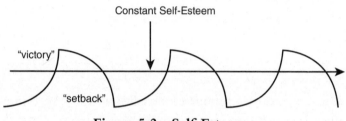

Figure 5.2   Self-Esteem

A quick search on Google results in over 500,000,000 hits on the word "presence." (Yes, over 500 *million.*) So let's try to simplify this.

We demonstrated earlier the need for high self-esteem along with high efficacy. Think of esteem as you would a muscle. It requires constant exercise to strengthen it and to avoid atrophy. Every day you have to build this esteem muscle just as you would visit a gym for your quads or triceps.

You can also think of esteem as a verb or action, which leads you to a noun—or condition—we'll call confidence. People with significant presence demonstrate high levels of confidence.

As you can see in Figure 5.2, many of us are confined to being as good or bad as our last victory or defeat. This is situational esteem, and it's a killer. Not only are we on this bumpy course, but our esteem is controlled largely by external forces—the competition, the environment, the family, and so forth.

However, when esteem is a constant, despite life's inevitable vicissitudes and curveballs, we control it internally. No matter how we perform, the result *doesn't affect our self-worth.* We know who we are. The current vernacular is "comfortable in our own skin." Hence, we're not thrown down the stairs simply because we lost a game or inconsolably glum if we weren't chosen for the team. Similarly, we're not convinced of our immortality or imperviousness just because we won or were successful or chosen.

What are the attributes of presence in a person?

- Well prepared and in possession of the facts and all sides—not just our own—of any issue.
- An effective use of language—including metaphor, vocabulary, examples, and inflection—to convey ideas.
- Brevity. People who possess the attribute of brevity are immediately and clearly understood. They tell people what they need to know *and not everything that they know.*
- A strong sense of humor (especially self-effacing humor) and adept storytelling to make a point.
- Generous. Generous people share credit, accept blame, and will always offer to pick up the check.
- A sense of proportion. People with a sense of proportion don't panic; they understand perspective and have global frames of reference. They try to avoid polarization.
- Finally, as previously noted, confidence. Confident people enter a room with grace. They smile. They are comfortable in being who they are.

Case Study

Everyone I've ever met who knows Bill Clinton has told me that he has tremendous presence. I spent some time with Democratic and political strategist James Carville when he was my guest speaker not long ago, and I asked him why this was so.[4]

Carville told me, as an example, that when Clinton entered an event or meeting, he looked around for the people who were

---

[4]Discussion with the author October 2014 in Palm Beach, Florida.

most uncomfortable, most junior, or most unlikely to be there, and headed straight for them. He'd strike up a conversation, and make them feel wonderful. Everyone in the room would be impressed. I've since tried to remind myself to do that whenever I can.

We feel that acquiring presence is a legitimate and important goal in the evolutionary journey (no matter what term we use to describe the behaviors or explain the impact). The key is self-esteem, that strong sense of worth that is undisturbed and undiminished by wins and losses, complaints and plaudits, ups and downs. Ironically, we're at our best when we are simply our best selves. Judy Garland said once, "Always be a first-rate version of yourself and not a second-rate version of someone else."[5]

But how does one do this in a world constantly trying to make us into someone else, interrupting or redirecting our journey, imposing significant normative pressures, and often rewarding counterproductive behaviors along the way?

Consistency in Turbulent Times

Your character and your esteem are reciprocal. They strengthen each other. (Or, they can undermine each other.) Peter Drucker wrote a fabulous book called *Managing in Turbulent Times*.[6] Today, a decade later, turbulent times are the norm. We might as well get used to them and get better at dealing with them.

Features of today's turbulent times include:

- No expectation of privacy
- Immediate and irretrievable communication
- Global applications and competition

---

[5] https://www.goodreads.com/author/quotes/179335.Judy_Garland.
[6] Peter F. Drucker, *Managing in Turbulent Times* (New York: HarperCollins, 2006).

- Rapidly advancing technology (sometimes helpful and sometimes not)
- Shifting demographics
- Remote learning
- Extensive extracurricular activities for kids
- Huge pressure on attention spans
- Virtual reality in business and personal pursuits

You can certainly add many more. How does one cope? Even with strong esteem, how do you progress, let alone hold your position, against these headwinds? What actions can you take to continue your journey in the directions you've plotted, slamming shut the watertight doors behind you?

Here is our recipe for being faithful and firm in your course during turbulent times (in other words, modern times):

1. *Create a support system.* We've seen too many people fail because their closest family and friends undermined them. When I tell you that you can't do something because I found that I couldn't do it, that's projection. You're no better than I am, right?

   You require people around you who can give you honest feedback when requested, and who buy into your journey. That may mean candid discussions with a partner, vulnerability among friends, and truthfulness with yourself. These people create a constant eye in the storm. If they are not of that persuasion, they will merely exacerbate the wind gusts and rain.

   You're responsible for creating your own support.

2. *Understand that behavior is more important than victories.* If you engage in consistently correct behavior, you'll be successful. It's far better to be gracious in winning and losing, for example, than to win constantly by manipulation and deceit, which will eventually do you in.

   You can't cement victories into your operating system, but you can cement behaviors. They become part of your unconscious competency, your automatic habits, and stand you in good stead in all circumstances. A person who's naturally generous will be so without thinking about it, gaining the respect of others without trying.

3. *Seek excellence, not perfection.* The futile search for perfection will kill success, because it is never achieved. No plane you've been on, no dinner you've consumed, no relationship you've developed, has ever been or will ever be perfect. Yet we procrastinate, delay, and postpone, holding out for an ideal that never materializes.

   Once you're content with excellence, you'll improve daily and will act daily with alacrity and intent. Your journey will speed up because you've accepted and embarked upon a good route, and have not waited for the (illusory) perfect route.

   Tom Brady and the New England Patriots were pretty dreadful through almost three quarters of the Super Bowl, but then went on to win in perhaps the most thrilling game of all time (and a record fifth Super Bowl win for Brady). They were far from perfect; they merely outplayed their opponents through perseverance and hard work.

4. *Learn when to fold and when to hold.* There is a time in many pursuits, no matter how worthy and cherished, when you no longer throw good money after bad. Poor gamblers seem to think that they can reverse luck if they just keep playing and, when they're ahead, don't know when to quit. (In Figure 5.1, it's the sector where they're happy but there's no meaning, just an addiction.)

   We've seen too many people endure bad bosses, poor relationships, unruly children, burdensome obligations, and other "necessary evils" to the point of depression. There is a time when you cannot change things, they will not get better on their own, and you need to take a sharp right turn to escape your predicament, as in Figure 5.3.

I once worked with a water treatment company that was a perpetual third in its market behind two behemoths. I told them to change

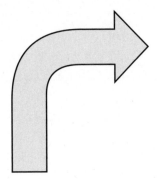

Figure 5.3   The Sharp Right Turn

their orientation to effluent management and recycling—the sharp right turn—and they were immediately number one in that new field!

On the other hand, I talked to a reporter with a major newspaper who complained at length about the hours, poor pay, lack of modern equipment, and tyrannical management. I suggested that he leave the work.

"Are you kidding?!" he yelled, "I love this job!"

If your viewpoint is based on your consistent level of high self-esteem, you'll find that the peaks and valleys are actually the turbulent times. Using the preceding recipe, your goal is to remain steady, to maintain your equilibrium through it all and allow your character and your presence to be paramount, guiding you through turbulent times, helping you continue on your journey, and allowing you to be at your imperfect best come hell or high water.

Assuming Formal and Informal Leadership

Formal leadership is hierarchical, with titles that indicate status (such as union steward, executive director, senior advisor, committee chair, etc.). Informal leadership is nonhierarchical and is often reflective of:

- Accomplishment (e.g., best salesperson)
- Respect (one who shares credit and accepts blame)
- Longevity

- Decision making (one who produces the best options)
- Team contribution (one who supports others)
- Trust (one who honors promises, deadlines, and commitments)
- Charisma (one who is exciting to be around)

It's possible to be a formal, hierarchical leader with none of these informal leadership qualities. Titles (or strings of initials after a name) don't make great leaders. So how to develop leadership skills? Some of it comes down to preparation. Here are some behaviors to aspire to and practice:

Share credit, accept blame: The recently coined, otherwise silly construction "my bad" is a lighthearted way to say "my fault." It's a step in the right direction. It's not avoidance, nor is it denial. It's acceptance with a cute phrase that softens the hit. I don't hear many people say "your bad." The best leaders we've seen tell their subordinates, peers, and superiors when they err and assure them that they will make it right. "My bad" is the latest iteration of "the buck stops here."

Many professional football quarterbacks buy a gift for their entire offensive line when they win an award. They know they wouldn't be recipients of any award if they were knocked on their backs on every play, and it's the offensive line that enables them to stay upright. There are many people around us keeping us upright! They don't necessarily need gifts but they do deserve credit.

Those endless award acceptance speeches at the Oscars, the Emmys, the CMAs, or the Tonys are attempts to share the credit with otherwise unseen and unknown supporters. I tend to forgive the delivery when I consider the intent.

Apologize: Admitting responsibility is one thing, but making an apology is another. The words "I'm sorry" or "I apologize" are often lost in the vagueness of "my bad" or "oops" or "not so good." Apologies bring catharsis to our souls and are a means of moving on, of expiating grudges and grievances.

There are three steps to a healthy apology:

1. *Admit the error or mistake as your fault.* Don't make excuses and don't try to deliver a rationale (e.g., you didn't give me all the information, I read the numbers wrong).
2. *Formally apologize with specifics.* "I'm very sorry I caused you to miss the party, and to waste the food you had prepared. I was thoughtless in being so late and not calling."
3. *Ask for forgiveness, make an offer of atonement, and move on.* "I hope you can forgive me, I'll do my best to never allow it to happen again, and if there's anything I can do right now to atone, just name it." Usually, people are happy with the apology or seek a modest reimbursement. Their anger subsides when faced with true contrition.

Strive for consensus, not victory. Consensus is something you can live with, not something you'd die for. The ability to facilitate disparate views and create a shared vision that all can support shows tremendous leadership strength.

   Are you trying to win and force the other person to lose, as in a debate or contest? Or are you looking for opportunities to create common ground that everyone can share and that will profit all concerned? Leadership is about inclusion and embrace, not polarization (which is why so much about politics is not true leadership).

Don't retreat from tough decisions. Sometimes, someone must be fired, or reprimanded, or transferred, or penalized. An unpopular project must be abandoned. Goals must be sacrificed. This occurs in business, families, education, nonprofits, the arts, and everyplace else. The longer these decisions are put off or ignored or delegated, the longer issues have to fester and become far more harmful.

   Most people who are fired are soon much happier than they were when they were dreading going into work each day fearing the worst. An obvious poor performance in the arts or on the playing field is best dealt with honestly, since everyone is well aware that it's happened.

The ability to accept accountability for tough decisions is the hallmark of great leadership, no matter what the environment.

Create and sustain discipline and organization: How adept are you at the following?

- Meeting deadlines
- Fulfilling your commitments
- Completing tasks rapidly
- Locating needed information quickly
- Planning your time
- Establishing correct priorities
- Assessing risk and reward potential
- Identifying and mobilizing resources
- Building teams appropriate to the tasks
- Making rapid, successful decisions
- Solving problems rapidly and correctly
- Creating new ideas and innovating

These are the specifics of organization and discipline. And remember this definition:

$$\text{Organization} + \text{Discipline} = \text{Speed}$$

Tomorrow's leaders will have to be faster than ever, whether formal or informal, temporary or permanent.

Coach others formally or informally: There is an increasingly popular school of thought that the primary coaches in any organization have to be the leaders—not outsiders certified by others, no matter how adept. (Remember, we are both coaches!) In families, we've found that coaching is far better than fiat. (When I confronted my father with his own rules transgressions, he always used to say, "Do as I say, not as I do!" I never found that convincing and never dared try it on my own kids.)

The teacher learns more than the student and the coach learns more than the teacher. Have you ever helped others who approached you for advice or techniques? Did the advice or technique improve their condition?

Congratulations, you're a coach! There is, perhaps, no more intrinsic aspect of leadership. And coaching isn't merely remedial. Great athletes, performers, writers, and others all use coaches. Self-improvement seems to have a governor, like a car designed not to exceed 150 miles per hour, even though it could theoretically do so. The investment people make in themselves provides the greatest return of any investment they can make.

To maximize that investment's return, we will always need a coach at critical junctures. Consequently, that should be a priority in your preparation for your future (or present) leadership roles.

The preceding are terrific practices to employ throughout your evolutionary journey, especially if you're likely to hold a leadership position somewhere down the line. But many people don't start thinking about leadership skills until they're thrust into a leadership role, when demands are coming at them thick and fast. In these high-stress, high-stakes environments, there is little time for focusing on change and personal development. Paradoxically, the more that is expected of you as a leader, the less time you have for learning—yet improving your leadership skills is more important than ever. With limited time, you have to learn on the job and ask those around you for help.

I (Marshall), with my colleague Howard Morgan, developed a leadership development model that has now been proven to work with thousands and thousands of people. This model consists of just eight steps, and it doesn't take a lot of time or preparation. I've seen many leaders fold these steps into their routines with little to no disruption.

1. *Ask:* Ask people, "How can I be a better _____ (manager, partner, team member, etc.)?" If you want to get better but don't know what you need to get better at, peruse the preceding list of leadership skills.

2. *Listen:* Listen to their answers.

3. *Think:* Think about their input. What does it mean?

4. *Thank:* Thank people for sharing their valuable feedback with you.

5. *Respond:* Respond positively when receiving input.

6. *Involve:* Involve the people around you to support your change efforts.

7. *Change:* Change isn't an academic exercise. Act on what you learn.

8. *Follow up:* Follow up regularly and stakeholders will notice the positive actions you're taking based on their input. This step is key in creating actual, measurable change!

We've found this process remarkably effective in developing leaders. Keep each step simple, positive, focused, and fast, and you will see results.[7]

Self-Assessment

We are somewhat more than halfway through the book, and have spent a great amount of time on the importance of character and evolution, particularly as related to present and future leadership in your evolutionary journey.

We both frequently take stock of our own journeys' progress. Unless you have metrics for success, it's almost impossible to assess whether you're doing well. There's an old sailor's maxim that says, "No wind is a good wind if you aren't sure of your port of call." An old Bob Newhart routine features a pilot out of London halfway across the Atlantic, announcing that he has good news and bad news. The good news is that the flight is two hours ahead of schedule. The bad news is that it will land in either New York or Buenos Aires.

---

[7] Frances Hesselbein, Marshall Goldsmith, and Richard Beckhard, *The Drucker Foundation: The Leader of the Future* (San Francisco: Jossey-Bass, 1997), pp. 227–237.

Case Study

I helped a CEO fire a vice president once by convincing the CEO that the subordinate was unhappy living with the constant threat of being terminated and the ostracism, and would be happier with a decent severance and freedom. The CEO thought he was sparing the vice president humiliation by keeping him around, despite his poor performance and inability to get along with his peers.

I helped another CEO to fire a rude, blasphemous sales vice president whom he felt it was his obligation to protect since he was the son of the former owner. I pointed out that the vice president's horrible behavior was considered by employees to be an extension of the CEO's behavior, since he wasn't stopping it. He fired the man almost immediately.

Tough decisions—often unpopular decisions—that are nevertheless made firmly and rapidly demonstrate high character. If you want your people to love you, try earning their respect first.

Here's a brief assessment. Take it now and see how you do:

To what extent are you sharing credit and accepting blame? In what areas can you share credit in the future on a consistent basis?

Do you owe someone an apology? If so, when will you deliver it? If not, would you be open to providing one if circumstances require it in the future?

Are you able to create common ground and goals for a variety of diverse viewpoints, bringing them together into a common purpose? What are the best situations for you to practice this skill?

Do you make tough decisions or do you procrastinate or ask someone else to make them? What tough decisions do you see on the horizon, and how will you prepare for them?

Rate yourself 1 (I need improvement), 2 (I'm good but not consistent), or 3 (I'm continually excellent) for the following skills (listed earlier in the chapter), then add up your score:

- Meeting deadlines
- Fulfilling your commitments
- Completing tasks rapidly
- Locating needed information quickly
- Planning your time
- Establishing correct priorities
- Assessing risk and reward potential
- Identifying and mobilizing resources
- Building teams appropriate to the tasks
- Making rapid, successful decisions
- Solving problems rapidly and correctly
- Creating new ideas and innovating

The only acceptable score for true leadership is 36!

Character is vital as a gyroscope for our behaviors and worldview. The elements of character are clear—we've described our choices in this chapter—and can be learned, mastered, improved upon, and sustained as your journey progresses. There is no sense in waiting for the right opportunity or believing the elements of character will magically appear with age.

Character determines ethical behavior in a world in which ethics are the bedrock for capitalism and honest, effective market transactions. It enables you to successfully apply influence and achieve that often cited but nevertheless elusive presence. It provides consistency in even turbulent times and supports both formal and informal leadership. It enables you to make the tough but necessary decisions that too many people ignore, avoid, or put off.

Lifestorming is about the journey you've embarked on to prepare the future you desire and deserve—admittedly a moving target, but a target in any case—so that the world doesn't make you into something else entirely. And that it can do readily if you're not paying attention, taking charge, and utilizing the internal control that is reciprocal with external influences (the world impacts us, we influence the world).

To refrain from this—to refuse to embark on the journey, or to choose a different and easier direction—is to surrender control. You've experienced this when you've held a grudge that the other party was unaware of: You've wasted time and energy being angry at someone else, and that person has wasted no time worrying about you. The wish to have said something yesterday or to get even when the opportunity arises or to let everyone know of your treatment is not a component of strong character. But the willingness to let go and learn from any experience, no matter how painful, is a huge aspect of character, growth, and the right direction in your journey.

The point is that we've all occasionally been on the wrong path at the wrong speed and realized that it didn't get us where we needed to go. I once told my daughter, who was very upset at some perceived slight, that "crying doesn't help."

My son, observing this interaction nearby, said to me later, "Actually, what *does* help?"

A strong character is all the help you'll need for yourself and for others.

6

Critical Abandonment (Knowing When to Hold and When to Fold)

The Dynamics of Keeping and of Changing

Americans are passionate consumers and acquirers of things. The *Los Angeles Times* once reported that our homes contain an average of 300,000 items![1] At the same time, we are fascinated with getting rid of our stuff. The book *The Life-Changing Magic of Tidying Up*, written by Japanese home organization expert Marie Kondo, is a global bestseller. Apparently, 4 million of us want help eliminating the objects in our lives that do not, as the book says, "spark joy."[2] This speaks volumes about our consumer culture, but it also reveals an underlying obsession with cyclical change: We purge the old to bring in the new. And we are hungry for expert advice about how to pull it off.

---

[1] Mary MacVean, "For Many People, Gathering Possessions Is Just the Stuff of Life," *Los Angeles Times*, March 21, 2014, http://articles.latimes.com/2014/mar/21/health/la-he-keeping-stuff-20140322.
[2] Marie Kondo, *The Life-Changing Magic of Tidying Up* (Tokyo: Sunmark Publishing, 2015), www.mariekondobooks.com.

As a consultant, I advise our clients in professional services to consider "firing" the bottom 10 to 15 percent of their clients every two years. That's because although many of these clients made sense at a different point in their growth and our own, they no longer provide support or are even profitable. In the corporate world as well, I advise that our clients triage their customers, so that the most attention can be paid to and the highest investment made in the most loyal and highest potential customers.

I would never advise abandoning *all* customers! And I don't advise you to abandon *all* habits. But some relationships are holding you back, and some people are taking advantage. Which relationships should you continue to develop, and which should you gently let go? In business, I recommend that customers be referred elsewhere when they:

- Are problem-prone and complain about trivial matters.
- Don't present any more potential business.
- Don't refer business.
- Are no longer profitable.
- Are engaged in unethical or questionable activities.
- No longer match your mission statement and values.

Similarly, there are analogous criteria to decide what relationships to hold and which to fold. First, let's examine the dynamic, as illustrated in Figure 6.1.

Before we talk about which relationships to let go of and which ones to keep, let's be clear about a few things. Of course we don't recommend that you jilt longstanding clients or old friends simply because they aren't your style anymore. Many of our successful clients have outpaced their peers in income and social status. The happiest among them know how to maintain old relationships without awkwardness. They gain more respect, not less, by keeping their old connections. I (Marshall) know a young man (who I'll call Jake) who started out as a struggling comedian and became quite successful in film and television. Even at the height of his fame, he always made time to pick up the phone and call his old comedy pals on their

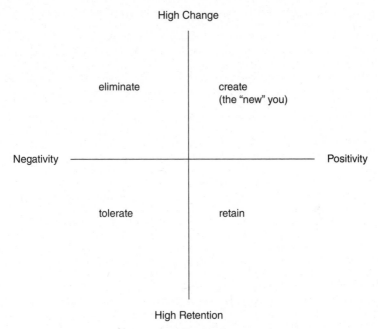

Figure 6.1   Critical Abandonment

birthdays. They already thought well of him (even if they were a little envious of his success), but those phone calls made them respect him even more.

So when we talk about relationships to *eliminate* (represented by the upper left-hand quadrant of Figure 6.1), we are talking about relationships that are consistently, poisonously negative, and are extremely unlikely to change. This category includes people who regularly belittle us, people consumed by addiction, or people who make dangerous ethical lapses that could compromise our livelihoods. It also represents relationships with groups that are bringing us down. We suggest dropping memberships in organizations that are downers, meant only for commiseration and cementing a sense of victimhood. We also suggest avoiding negative or depressing publications. If quitting them cold turkey is hard to do, realize that you can achieve just about the same effect by drastically restricting your time with them in frequency, duration, and intensity.

In professional settings, it's not terribly hard to cut ties with people or groups who are bringing us down. I had a client who I'll call Brad, who attended a series of meetings I led. Brad was getting to be a problem, angrily interrupting others. I suggested that he find another group to attend, and his angry outbursts were instantly a thing of the past. The group dynamic immediately changed for the better.

Eliminating a long-term, personal relationship is much harder, of course. Sometimes it isn't even possible. We are stuck with some people for life. These relationships bring us into the lower left quadrant of the figure, where we identify those negative forces we decide we have to *accept*. We basically make peace with the relationship or circumstance.

We sometimes must accept coworkers who complain or lash out. Perhaps the person comes with the job. Many people love their work so much that they'll accept a boss who does this. (Yet if you don't love your work, that's a futile tactic.) It's almost impossible to ignore a hovering mother or domineering father (or vice versa). Unless we decide we're going to cut them off forever, we have to find a way to accept the feuds at family gatherings—or the other trouble they tend to cause. We can anticipate these dynamics, prepare for them, and be at peace in our tolerance of them. If we don't accept the things we can't change, we'll forever be stressed and unhealthy.

This is easier said than done—we know! But it is possible. I (Marshall) have a single friend I'll call Joe, whose elderly mother moved into his home with little warning. She spent the days shuffling around in a bathrobe, making dire predictions about the future and bemoaning the state of the world. Surprisingly, Joe's reaction was to laugh good-naturedly, as if she were making jokes instead of complaining. He had decided to treat her rants as amusing (and to be honest, her pessimistic tirades did sound a little bit like a *Saturday Night Live* sketch). His good humor never rubbed off on her, but it did keep him in decent spirits until she finally found a more permanent living arrangement.

And that leads us to the lower right quadrant, where we assertively *retain* relationships that are inherently valuable. These are positive relationships that we want to keep. They have been and are rewarding in their own right.

Many of us have had childhood friends with whom we retain relationships, whether close or distant. Some are quite valuable in a practical sense, in that these people know us and the journey we've completed thus far. Some are valuable emotionally, because they help us retain the perspective often lost with success, changed circumstances, and our evolutionary journey. Both of us are lucky to be in long and happy marriages. The value of these partnerships cannot be overstated.

In the upper right quadrant we see the "new you." This is the area of positive, proactive change, in which we *create* new relationships. While the preserving sustains us, the creating enables us to grow. We need people who can stretch us, provide new viewpoints, supply differing perspectives, and challenge our beliefs. (Remember, in sealing the watertight doors, we often must adjust our viewpoints.) Creating new relationships can mean joining new clubs, taking up new pursuits (hobbies, sports, causes), becoming more involved in the community, introducing yourself to others, or identifying with whom you'd like to hang out.

For example, if you want to be a technical expert, hang out with technical experts. If you want to be a community leader, hang out with community leaders. If you want to be a thought leader, hang out with thought leaders.

We think it's useful to *purposely* determine the relationships to eliminate, accept, retain, and create. Think of two people who are in your life now—or who should be in your life, in the case of the "create" quadrant)—who belong in each category:

Eliminate

1. _____

2. _____

Accept

1. _____

2. _____

Retain

1. _____

2. _____

Create

1. _____

2. _____

Now answer this: What action is required for each?

Eliminate

1. _____

2. _____

Accept

1. _____

2. _____

Retain

1. _____

2. _____

Create

1. _____

2. _____

There is more to these quadrants than relationships, of course. You could ask yourself the same questions and formulate appropriate actions for:

- Avocations
- Occupations
- Possessions
- Travel destinations
- Memberships
- Time allocation
- Philanthropy and support
- Community involvement
- Family obligations
- Hobbies

In all of these areas, there are probably a few things each of us could eliminate and be better off. If we don't, we wind up in a psychological hoarder's den, filled with so many old habits and outdated self-concepts that we hardly have room to move. We can get so weighted down by life's accretions that we have no energy or space to create anything new.

Sometimes (often, in fact) we don't even know we're doing this. That's why the preceding exercise is so helpful. By naming things we can eliminate, accept, retain, and create, we begin to think hard about what really matters to us. The act of eliminating can seem like the most drastic and frightening aspect of this process, but when you get rid of something you truly do not need the effect is liberating. I (Marshall) am a Buddhist. This concept of freeing oneself by letting go is central to the Buddhist tradition.

And yet it is a hard concept for highly successful people to grasp. Earlier, I mentioned that some successful leaders like to win so much that it's almost an addiction. To gauge the severity of this addiction, I present them with the following case study:

> You want to go to dinner at restaurant X. Your spouse, partner, or friend wants to go to dinner at restaurant Y. You have a heated argument. You end up at restaurant Y—not your choice. The food tastes awful. The service is terrible.

> Option A: Critique the experience. Point out that your dining companion was wrong. Explain that this terrible mistake could have been avoided if you had made the decision.

> Option B: Shut up. Eat the stupid food. Try to enjoy it. Have a nice evening.

> What would you do? What should you do?

Seventy-five percent of my clients fail themselves by saying that they would critique the food. They readily admit that what they should do is shut up and enjoy the evening. There's nothing to be gained here by critiquing and complaining.

How do you take a more thoughtful approach to such situations and keep your desire to win in check? Before speaking, take a deep breath and ask yourself these three questions:

1. *Why am I trying so hard to win this point?* Our excessive need to win is often driven more by our personal need to prove how smart we are than by our altruistic desire to help others. In the

long run, no one is ever impressed with our need to display our own brilliance.

2. *Is this debate worth my time and energy?* You are probably already too busy. Is this argument the most efficient way to help you achieve your goals? If so, go for it! If not, drop it.

3. *What is more important, the point that I am trying to win or my relationship with this human being?* In many cases it will become obvious to you that the benefit of winning small points is less important than the cost of damaging valued relationships.

Win the big ones. Let go of the rest.

Adjustments and Accommodations

Eliminating things from our lives isn't—and shouldn't be—a cut-and-dry task. We suggest doing it gradually and in most cases not stopping abruptly. (Stopping smoking cold turkey is marvelous if one can do it. Ending a long-term relationship or interaction is another story.)

A woman named Roxanne was a strong supporter of a professional trade association. She attended the monthly meetings, went on to serve on the board for several terms, and served as president for two years. She actively solicited new members, settled disputes, and created great energy. But her own business was growing far faster than her colleagues' businesses, and she had truly outgrown the group.

She was loyal to it, and saw a diminished role as a betrayal, until she evaluated her actions in light of the above discussion. She realized that what was once a source of great energy had become a drain. Where once she learned, now she almost solely taught. Where she had once had fun creating new fund-raisers and activities, she now had neither time nor interest to do so.

She declined to continue to serve on the board, reduced her attendance from monthly to quarterly, and consequently interacted with other members far less between meetings. In this way she could reduce her affiliation while keeping on the road to elimination (which she has since done) without damage or insult or bad feelings. But without this coaching, she probably wouldn't have made that progress, instead falling victim to a distorted sense of obligation and loyalty.

The same perspective is useful in considering what we need to simply accept. I (Marshall) have developed a simple formulation that helps my coaching clients decide whether they should leap into battle or make peace with a situation. Follow this formulation, and you will dramatically shrink your daily volume of stress, unpleasant debate, and wasted time. I phrase it as a question:

A - Glume — A.I, W.A.T.T.

Am I willing
At this time
To make the investment required
To make a positive difference
On this topic?

It pops into my head so often each day that I've turned the first five words into an acronym AIWATT (it rhymes with "say what"). Perhaps you're thinking, "I don't need to repeat a simple question to know which battles are worth fighting." But I believe that all of us need exactly this kind of help. I have long contended that relying on structure—even something as simple as the AIWATT question—is key to changing our behavior.

This 19-word question creates a split-second delay in our potentially prideful, cynical, judgmental, argumentative, and selfish responses to our environment. The delay gives us time to consider a more positive response. AIWATT helps us when a trigger creates an impulse—and before we exhibit behavior that we may later regret. The text deserves close parsing:

"Am I willing" implies that we are exercising volition—taking responsibility—rather than surfing along the waves of inertia that otherwise rule our day. We are asking, "Do I really want to do this?"

"At this time" reminds us that we're operating in the present. Circumstances may differ later on, perhaps demanding a different response. The only issue is what we're facing now.

"To make the investment required" reminds us that responding to others is work, an expenditure of time, energy, and opportunity. And, like any investment, our resources are finite. We are asking, "Is this really the best use of my time?"

"To make a positive difference" places the emphasis on the kinder, gentler side of our nature. It's a reminder that we can help create a better us or a better world. If we're not accomplishing one or the other, why are we getting involved?

"On this topic" focuses us on the matter at hand. We can't solve every problem. The time we spend on topics for which we can't make a positive difference is stolen from topics where we can.

AIWATT offers a simple cost-benefit analysis: Is this battle worth fighting? If not, accept the situation and look for where you can really make a difference.

The AIWATT concept also applies to what we want to preserve. Retaining might seem like the easiest of the four elements, but as anyone who has been in a long-term relationship knows, keeping something in good condition takes time, energy, focus, and work. Bob Dylan famously wrote, "He not busy being born is busy dying." If you're not investing in something, it will start to decay. Decide what it is you want to preserve (your family relationships, your marriage, your job, or your ability to speak a foreign language or play a musical instrument, for example). Then decide if you're willing to do the work required to maintain them.[3]

As coaches, we know that the last action, creating, generates the most excitement. This is where dramatic transformations happen— where the shy person learns to speak up, the impatient person learns to slow down and listen, or the heavy person finally sheds the unwanted pounds. The novelty is exciting—but be careful that all of the changes you make really are for the better. Sometimes people enter our lives

---

[3] Marshall Goldsmith and Mark Reiter, *Triggers: Creating Behavior That Lasts— Becoming the Person You Want to Be* (New York: Crown Publishing, 2015).

Zeno's Paradox —
If Everyday you Cover Half
The Distance To your Goal — You'll Never
Reach Your Goal

who are new—high change—but are not positive. Not every new person or circumstance is desirable. "New" is not synonymous with "beneficial." In fact, new can be negative. This is a systemic problem with kids, where normative pressures often force them into new relationships that are dysfunctional. Kids sometimes smoke, drink, do drugs, or engage in criminal acts because their new friends are doing it and kids are afraid of rejection for not engaging in the in behavior.

Many of us seek out new relationships or behaviors because we think they will make us happy in the future. Of course, many of the achievements we pursue really do create happiness. For example, rewarding careers, stable marriages, and better interpersonal habits create an ongoing source of well-being. But realize that happiness is a choice, always attainable in the present. Previously, we exhorted you to be happy now. Let your new relationships and personal transformations add to and reinforce that happiness, as opposed to trying to fill a well of sadness and disappointment. The fact is, you won't be happy if you believe there's a destination point for being happy. Zeno's famous paradox states that if every day you cover half the distance to your goal, you'll never reach the goal.

Instead, aim for evolutionary reinvention. Your journey should be one of continually becoming a new, improved person, in part by assertively and proactively creating your new world (upper right quadrant). Just as a company can't cut its way to growth—most cost-cutting initiatives don't achieve anywhere near projected savings but they do significantly lower productivity—we can't reinvent ourselves by relying on accepted and retained relationships (or even by effectively eliminating those we must). We have to actively create.

Between us, we've been to over 100 countries, written nearly 100 books, worked with hundreds of firms and tens of thousands of people, and provided hundreds of millions of dollars in improvements, savings, and growth. That's because we've consciously and emphatically created the new. And we're still doing so every day.

Are you?

Here are some questions to consider as you attempt to do so:

- What life do I envision for myself a year from now?
- If I had the chance, whom would I like to meet and develop a relationship with?
- What am I accepting as a necessary evil or as an obligation I impose on myself?
- Am I using my own metrics for progress and success or someone else's?
- Which of my quadrants is most heavily weighted at the moment, and how can I put more emphasis on creating?
- If I look back a year, will I have made the progress I anticipated?

GPS and Roadside Assistance

No new journey of consequence occurs without occasional wrong turns, unanticipated delays, unexpected distractions, mechanical problems, need for fuel, and even minor accidents. Expecting a constant smooth ride is unrealistic, and we shouldn't become disappointed, or worse, abandon the journey if we face obstacles and need to take detours.

We've both been on a constant journey and reached tens of thousands of others on theirs. Here are some of the travel problems you'll face. The key is to not break down entirely and to not pursue a totally wrong direction.

You're Traveling at the Wrong Speed — PACE

The journey is about moving as rapidly as you can *while retaining control*. Creeping along in the slow lane is tantamount to merely sticking your toes in the water when the point is to swim (and maybe even make waves). While you don't want to lose control on the turns or hit someone in front of you, you also don't want to see everyone pass you by.

Set aggressive metrics. If you want to write a book, serve as school board committee chair, or travel to the other side of the world, don't just create a misleading bucket list with no accountabilities. Create an aggressive timeline with milestones: for example, run for school committee next election, create a book proposal by April, talk to a travel agent tomorrow about an Asian tour.

The key here is to move as rapidly as you can while retaining control (of finances, time, relationships, and so forth). Prudent risk is fine. Gambling is not.

You're Using the Wrong Maps and Directions

If we put the wrong address into GPS it will take us to the wrong destination, no matter how rapidly. If we use someone else's map, which may have worked for her or him, it may be a destination inappropriate for us. (Think about our earlier discussions about people who chose careers because of parental and outside influences, not their own passions and talents.)

While our ultimate vision may be (and should be) a moving target, we need to identify and narrow down the possibilities. Steve Jobs and Bill Gates sought to be technology pioneers. Michael Jordan and Larry Bird wanted to be basketball players. We've mentioned how Shaquille O'Neill and Michael Strahan have successfully changed their maps.

In what do you want to excel, not merely exist? In medicine, business, teaching, law enforcement, entertainment, athletics, design? For now, what is the likely look of your future landscape so that you can begin plotting the right direction on the right map?

And you have to think big. No one goes to the Olympics with the mantra "Go for the bronze"! What's the general destination you want to insert into your personal GPS?

Your Vehicle Isn't in the Best Shape for the Trip

You need fuel and effective maintenance. You require high performance tires and a well-tuned engine.

speed

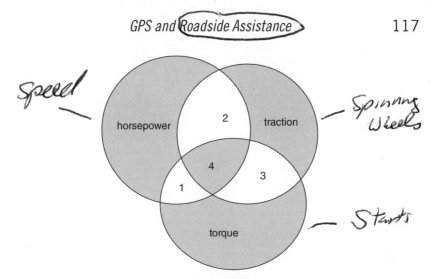

Spinning Wheels

Starts

Figure 6.2   The Vehicle on the Journey

Are you physically fit for your journey? Are you well rested, healthy, and have high energy? Are you mentally fit? Are you optimistic and enthusiastic? Are you so impassioned that a minor delay is tolerable and a brief detour is exciting? Or does any kind of mishap and unplanned event send you to a rest stop?

Your journey has to be one of self-sufficiency. That means you must constantly acquire new skills and new behaviors, just as a car needs gas and oil (or electrical charges). You need to seal the watertight doors so that you don't slip into reverse, erasing your gains. You need traction on the road, as well as torque and horsepower.

If you have horsepower and torque but no traction (condition 1 in Figure 6.2) your wheels will spin. You'll be involved with failure work and won't get a grip on your plans. Under condition 2, you may have traction and speed, but without torque you won't have very fast starts. Others will readily move ahead of you when you start at equal points. And if you have traction and torque (condition 3) but no horsepower (speed) you will lose the race to others who are faster.

You need all three elements:

1. The knowledge to give you traction
2. The awareness to give you torque
3. The enthusiasm to give you speed

My son, in his earlier years, always had great ideas (the electric toothbrush, automatic garage openers, and so forth) and I always had to alert him that someone else had already thought of it or had arrived there already. Of course, he was 10 at the time.

What's your excuse?

You Abuse the Vehicle

We're familiar with workaholics and people who put in long hours because they're afraid not to (can't leave while the boss is still there, even though the boss is making 10 times your income). There are professional paths that are brutal, such as trying to make partner in a law firm or in an accounting practice, or the path to becoming a physician with its insane sleepless periods and burnout. To me, the interns often look worse than the patients they are attending.

We've seen parents of both genders working a 60-hour week, leading a scout troop, helping with homework, chauffeuring to extracurricular activities, performing volunteer work, and serving on boards of nonprofits. Their willingness to contribute is admirable, but doing too much may do more harm than good. Pace your life. You can't help others unless you help yourself. As we said before, that's why the airlines tell you to put your own oxygen mask on first.

We see burnout all the time. We've stipulated that you should go as fast as you can *while possessing complete control*. You don't want to wipe out on the turns or hit a tree. That's why we don't call it a revolutionary journey, but an evolutionary one. Eagerness is fine, impatience is not. Prudent risk makes sense, tossing the dice doesn't. We talked earlier about granting yourself permission and assuming permission. But don't give yourself permission to be reckless.

Staying the Course

We'll conclude this chapter by emphasizing that change is exciting if you allow it to be, and controllable if you prepare for it. Avoiding a systems failure and providing for the retention of the valuable and abandonment of the obsolete is the guiding principle.

The new you is an ongoing phenomenon. Most of us experience success in some areas of life and find it elusive in others. Some of us are brilliant with finances but not romantic relationships, for instance. Others are great at staying in physical shape but struggle to get ahead in a professional setting. To achieve our full potential, we should take time to grow in every aspect of our lives.

The evolutionary journey has to be holistic. It involves growth as a person, not as a specialist. Our personal lives feed our careers and our careers feed our personal lives. An effective exercise is to ask ourselves what kind of people we wish to be in a year—as we proceed on our journey—and what's required to arrive there. But these can't be ambiguous goals (I want to be a better person, I want to be more positive). They should be specific and related to where we are today, improving on our current conditions. You can choose the areas and topics for improvement. Figure 6.3 provides a sample of how this might look for your ongoing metrics.

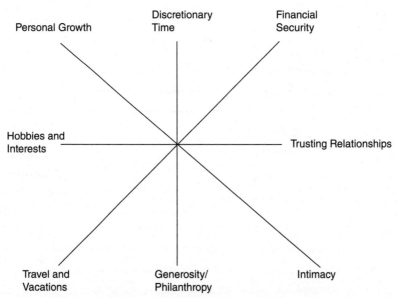

Figure 6.3 Personal Growth Metrics

Assume that the middle point of each line has a value of 0 and that the outer edges have a value of 10. Mark where you are in each category, allowing for the fact that you should adjust the sample categories we've provided to reflect your own priorities.

In other words, if you are assigning a value to financial security and you deem that a 10 would be having a year's expenses in a bank account, saving 15 percent of your total income, and maximizing your total contributions to deductible retirement plans—where are you now? If midway, give yourself a 5. If close to that ideal, make it an 8.

"Trusting relationships" might mean people around you who you know will tell you the truth, good or bad; whom you can trust for very personal advice; with whom you're comfortable partnering in business deals or vacations; and so forth. To what extent do you have these relationships now, if the conditions we've just described merit a 10?

It may be you have a 10 in some categories and a 0 in others. That doesn't matter. What does matter are these four questions:

1. Specifically, which categories are important to me? (You might require more or fewer lines.)
2. What constitutes a 10 (highly satisfying or effective) in each category?
3. In all candor, where am I today?
4. *What, specifically, do I have to do to move from my existing point to the goal I desire in each category?*

This is how you stay the course on your evolutionary journey. You create specific goals and metrics, understanding that the factors on the axes might change over time, that your ratings may change, and/or that your ultimate goal may become more challenging. That's part of growth. *As we grow, the bar gets higher and higher.*

We've found that this kind of schematic is useful when reviewed regularly and discussed with others we trust (especially partners). Because we often lose a sense of our priorities due to squeaky wheels or others' objectives, or due to the inevitable fire that's raging at work, we tend to lose sight of our own priorities and needs. Revisiting the chart helps us to refocus.

In addition, it assists us in assigning resources and creating priorities. As we've said before, time and money aren't *really* resources. They are priority decisions about where we invest our existing time and money, and future time and money. The spokes in the chart can and should help us determine where those investments should be made, because without the investments (specific actions) we cannot make progress toward a value of 10.

So this is how you abandon what's not needed; gain traction, torque, and speed; decide what to eliminate, accept, retain, and create. This puts you on the right road and enables you to stay the course.

Let's assume you're getting there. What's the next step in the journey?

7 | The New You

For the sake of argument, let's say that you are succeeding on your evolutionary journey. You've established goals that are unique to you, mastered the art of metamorphosis, and become a more successful human being in pretty much every area of life. The good news is that you've come this far. Congratulations! The news that is less good is that this is no time to rest on your laurels. We have observed over many years that achieving success does not immediately or automatically make life easier. Instead, it usually creates new challenges—often ones we didn't anticipate. Negative emotions and misplaced priorities can still sabotage our accomplishments and reverse our hard-won progress. We're especially vulnerable to these mistakes when we're in a new situation—a new job, a new relationship, or even a new state of awareness or understanding. If you know the potential pitfalls, you can avoid them.

Overcoming Fear

I've found that most people are afraid of things they often can't even articulate. We hear of fight or flight, and we should probably add to that, fright.

It's prudent and wise to be afraid of truly alarming situations: a person with a gun, an approaching tornado, a careening car. Yet we've seen people tremble uncontrollably in nonthreatening circumstances: addressing a group, entering a dark room, looking down from a great height. For children, this is common and understandable, but for adults with a body of knowledge and a lifetime of experiences, not so much. Leaders who have been promoted are often called upon to act boldly, and their behavior will face more scrutiny than before they were promoted. A fear of public speaking or hesitation on a key decision can be fatal to their careers during the pivotal early stages of their new positions.

Case Study

When I was 10 I was on a Little League baseball team, and all the parents showed up for the first game of the season. I wasn't a starter, but was inserted as a pinch hitter in the middle of the game.

I was so nervous, so scared of embarrassing myself, that my hands and legs were shaking. I struck out on three successive pitches, my swing never coming remotely close to the ball. It was as if my limbs were out of my control.

Later, I deeply regretted that fact that I never gave myself a chance. My irrational fear (What was *really* the worst thing that could happen?) had undermined any chance for success.

Three years later, having experience in the league and in playing, I made the All-Star team based on my hitting.

As mentioned, I always thought my son was afraid of the dark, and his stock reply was:

"Oh, I'm not afraid of the dark, I'm afraid of what might *be* in the dark!"

The dark is an area without light, and it's often created by our own refusal to allow the light in. We engage in false beliefs and are too easily persuaded by others who warn us of the dangers. Thus, a new job, a different routine, or a different relationship becomes the dark. Every journey has some dark. The idea is to both shed light and to be comfortable when it's truly dark.

Why are people fearful? Fear usually comes in the following varieties:

- *Fear of failure:* "I'm supposed to be the expert. What if my opinions are contradicted by someone who is respected?"
- *Fear of ridicule:* "What if I miss the putt that decides the match with everyone watching?"
- *Fear of falling short of standards set by others:* "I've done well, but my performance is nowhere near the performance of my older sister."
- *Fear of disappointing others, especially parents:* "My parents always told everyone I'd be a brilliant attorney, but what if I don't pass the bar exam? What if I'd rather be a teacher?"
- *Irrational fear or superstition:* "That room looks spooky. I don't want to go in there."
- *Fear of ostracism by peers:* "If my friends find out how I voted, they'll never talk to me again."

We fear for these reasons and others, usually irrationally. For example, an audience *hopes the speaker is successful and is initially quite supportive.* People don't want to go home and brag that they just wasted two hours watching a speaker fail. They'd prefer to say they've just spent time with a great speaker. But many speakers behave as though they're entering enemy territory!

There are two basic types of extreme fear:

1. *Choking.* This occurs when you know what has to be done but you can't bring yourself to do it well. It is my Little League experience—I could swing the bat, but I couldn't hit the ball. It's the person with the last-second chance to make the winning shot. The great athletes seldom choke because they enjoy playing under pressure and do it often. Delivering a speech only a few times a year doesn't provide the same preparation as doing it often.

2. *Panic.* This occurs when you no longer remember what to do. When I learned to scuba dive, the instructors beat into me the fact that if my regulator (whence comes the oxygen) failed for any reason, I could simply sweep back my right arm in an arc and bring forward a second, reserve regulator. We practiced it endlessly. But if, at 40 feet down, your regulator malfunctions and you panic, you will forget the arm motion entirely and die. It's not that you'll do it poorly (choke), it's that you won't be able to do it at all.

Have you seen people on the job who throw the equivalent of a gutter ball in bowling? They are choking. Have you seen people who draw a blank completely, and don't know what to do with the ball next? They are panicked.

In our journey, the unknown and the dark are inevitable companions at times. How do we overcome fear? Fortunately, there are highly pragmatic techniques that we've learned from thousands of clients:

Familiarize yourself with the environment: As a speaker, I always walk the stage before I speak to get acquainted with the feel and dimensions. If I can't do it immediately before I'm introduced, I'll do it in the morning or at lunch. (I'm not afraid of the dark but what might be in the dark.) Find out what's likely to be in the dark so that there are no unknowns to fear. The same holds true for sales meetings, travel, and sports.

Visualize what you can't familiarize: I've often pictured a prospect's office and whether we will sit across the desk from each other or on comfortable furniture in the room. I've visualized how to teach a program, and how to negotiate a deal. There are remarkably few options in most situations, and if you visualize the most likely (e.g., you're not going to stand in the prospect's office), you will familiarize yourself and gain the comfort required to overcome any fear.

Consider precedent: Ask if you've ever done something similar to what you're now considering: begun a new job, served on a committee or board, accepted a regimen. If you're expected to begin a health regimen due to an illness, and you're fearful of not being able to remain faithful to it, think of times when you were able to apply great discipline and the similarities between the situations. I always ask people, "Has anyone ever done this under similar circumstances?" The answer is almost always yes. If that's the case, why can't you do it?

Conquer fear with offense, not defense: Defense seldom wins a game (because it usually can't score points) and doesn't provide for movement. Hence, it can't contribute adequately to the journey. The phrase "put a stake in the ground" comes from the ancient Aztecs who would stake their ankles to the ground and either prevail or die because they could not retreat. The problem was that they also denied themselves the opportunity to rapidly pursue a fleeing enemy.

Call for the ball! Champions want to have the ball when the pressure is on and the game is on the line. Don't duck and hope it won't be you. Call for it. Your boldness in accepting that pressure will offset a missed shot, and you might just make the shot.

Hang out with bold people: Spend your time with people who seek opportunities and create innovation, not those who hide under their desks or say, "Let the other guy do it." Peer pressure can work in positive ways, so find people who overcome fear, are none the worse for the wear, and can set the precedents you need to go boldly forward.

Overcoming fear is much easier when you know the causes of your fear and can eliminate them or rationalize them. The ability to laugh at yourself is an important component—not so much when you've panicked underwater, but certainly when you've missed the ball with everyone watching. They can't laugh at you if you're laughing with them.

Banishing Guilt

Guilt is the belief that you have culpability. You feel terrible because:

- You did something that you should not have done.
- You have something that you should not have.
- You failed to do something.
- You failed to get something.

That pretty much covers the waterfront.

Guilt has become a verb: "Let's guilt him into doing it." Anyone who has had a caring mother has experienced the "You'd know more if you called more" kind of guilt trip. My wife, trying to please my grandmother, made her the tea she preferred early in our marriage. "How nice," smiled my grandmother, "a half a cup of tea. . . ."

We consume ourselves with guilt to the point that we sacrifice our own objectives. Yet that seldom makes us feel much better. Recall the oxygen mask principle: You can't help others effectively if you don't help yourself first. But guilt co-opts the ability to help yourself. Guilt encourages us—and even forces us—to:

- *Be too permissive with children.* We don't want our children to feel deprived. We want them to feel accepted by their peers (normative pressure). We don't want to be seen as overbearing parents, because that's not modern or hip. So we manage to still create problems for them by not enforcing discipline or creating accountability.

- *Sacrifice important personal goals.* The boss needs me, so I must stay later at the office even if I miss dinner with the family. The team needs me, and I'm going to have to delay our vacation and see if we can get our deposit back.
- *Enable others' spurious demands.* My cousin is not the right choice for this job, but he needs the money and we are family. I couldn't face him or his wife if I didn't offer him the position.
- *Abandon important relationships.* I don't know how I can ever face my friend again after what I've done (or failed to do).
- *Refrain from improving one's life or having good experiences.* I don't deserve go to Paris for vacation because others don't have that luxury.

Guilt saps energy and undermines talent. It kills risk taking, innovation, and creativity. Guilt is a giant mediocrity engine, reducing those afflicted with it to a lowest common denominator. It's the quicksand you may encounter along your journey. You are far better off avoiding it than attempting to pull yourself out of it. Here's how to avoid it:

- *If you've done something or failed to do something that causes pain to others, apologize.* Be specific: "I should not have left the reservations to the last minute and I'm sorry we have to travel overnight. It's my fault and I won't let it happen again." Feeling guilty doesn't help the aggrieved party in the least. Apologizing isn't an anodyne, but it's helpful.
- *Do not allow others to thrust guilt upon you.* Become adept at explaining why you can't do something and adopt a Teflon attitude. "I can't serve on the committee because I can't afford the time during my busy season, and I am already making a cash contribution." (Or, just say "no" with no excuse at all.)
- *Use the right metrics.* If you deserve something, you deserve it. Whether others have it or not is immaterial. Talent, skill, and achievement determine your ability to succeed and invest in

yourself. There is no requirement to conform to friends, neighbors, or critics. There may be people who don't have what you have, but that's not because you've denied them.

- *Examine your guilt.* What's the source of your guilt? How long have you been guilty and about what? If your guilt stems from a relationship or a person in the past, it may be hard to repair. That's why it's best to restore and rebuild those family relationships that you're feeling guilty about while all are still present. Too many people have felt guilty about the last words they said to someone, not realizing *they would be the last words.*

Guilt is akin to depression in that it masks talent. So long as you're feeling guilty you will never perform at optimal productivity, nor will you ever be entirely happy. (If you just thought, "No one has a right to be entirely happy," you're exhibiting guilt!)

There are three paradigms of guilt: commission, omission, and condition.

1. *Commission:* Commission is when you've made an error that has caused harm or inconvenience. These acts can be intentional or accidental. In either case, an apology is appropriate, along with a sincere promise of better self-control or awareness in the future. If you find it hard to break the cycle of doing bad things and then feeling guilty about them, seek help from a qualified coach or therapist. This type of guilt is a powerful destructive force if left unchecked.

2. *Omission:* Omission happens when you fail to do something necessary. Our society considers this a serious sin; for example, our justice system holds people accountable for doing nothing to stop or report crimes. On a less drastic level, failing to keep a commitment—such as a birthday or anniversary date—can create tremendous guilt. The remedy: Get organized and tune in to the people around you. The first thing I do with a new year's calendar is to write in my wife's and kids' birthdays and our wedding anniversary.

3. *Condition:* Some of us receive awards. Or win a contest. Or get a great job that fulfills a dream. However, there are those who feel no one should have any more than they do, even if they don't deserve something, and who will try to make you feel guilty. (In Australia this is called the tall poppy syndrome, meaning that any poppy standing taller than the others should be cut back.) In these cases you have to resist the guilt trip. You've done nothing wrong. Your success denies no one else. The condition of guilt will otherwise plague you your entire life as you succeed, and you won't fully enjoy your good fortune.

Ending Shame

The practice of executive coaching introduced corporate culture to an exciting new idea: the end of shame.

Under the guidance of a coach, it's okay to admit what you don't know and ask for help. My (Marshall's) coaching process brings my clients' areas for improvement into the light through a process of accumulating confidential feedback from their key stakeholders (colleagues, direct reports, and board members, for example). If that sounds terrifying, it's because most of us have been conditioned to hide our flaws for fear of punishment, reprisal, or a rival seizing a competitive advantage.

A good coach takes away that fear and uses feedback and self-analysis to guide clients toward positive and lasting behavioral change. The process works—which is one reason that I have seen the perception of coaching shift over the last three decades: Instead of a punishment, it's now a mark of prestige to have a coach. It means you're probably going places in your career.

What I find so remarkable about my friend and colleague Alan Mulally is that he put these ideas about ending shame into practice across an entire organization—and in an intense, high-stakes setting. When he took over as Ford's CEO in 2006, the company was in dire straits, with market share down 25 percent since 1990 and its very existence threatened by the Great Recession.

The story of how Alan turned Ford around is now well documented. The company was the only Big Three automaker to emerge from the recession without a government bailout. When Alan retired from Ford in 2014, *Fortune* magazine ranked him as the third greatest leader in the world, behind only Pope Francis and Angela Merkel.

One important thing that Alan did early on was to effectively eliminate shame. Up to that point, meetings at Ford were notoriously vicious, with executives publicly sparring or avoiding each other altogether by fiddling with their BlackBerrys. Alan rooted out those problems through his brilliantly simple Business Plan Review program, which made meetings highly structured. Executives had to introduce themselves and report on their progress according to a precise formula (and no BlackBerrys were allowed).

In this much calmer environment, he encouraged his reports to be honest about their problems. Instead of bravado, he encouraged them to show humility and admit when they needed help. He did this by modeling the behavior himself—the hallmark of a truly great leader. Alan was not ashamed of what he didn't know, or of what he had or hadn't done. He simply reported on the condition of the company with an attention to detail befitting his background as an engineer. When he didn't know how to fix a problem, he wasn't afraid to ask for help.

It sounds simple, and it is. But it takes tremendous courage to be so forthright—so unashamed—especially in a situation like the one he faced at Ford: fixing one of our nation's biggest companies on the brink of collapse in an industry that serves as a backbone of that nation's economy. When the world is watching and the stakes are high, a lesser leader would have armed himself with ego. Alan chose the other path.

I believe that his approach has the potential to do tremendous good in settings beyond Ford, which is why Alan and I are now working together to develop leadership teams at a wide range of organizations.

Overcoming fear, guilt, and shame go a long way toward creating the new you. It's like removing drag and making a vehicle more aerodynamic for the journey. Then we're on the road to higher self-worth.[1]

Maintaining High Self-Worth

As we've previously noted, self-worth is like a muscle that has to be flexed and used regularly. Muscles atrophy when not in use.

An important aspect of self-worth is believing in the worth of others. I try never to approach anyone—in either business or social settings—with negative expectations. It's dysfunctional to be cynical with every new person you encounter. I give them the benefit of the doubt. A tiny percentage of them disappoint me, but I try not to let their shortcomings color my perception of all people.

Thus, acceptance and forgiveness are the reciprocals of our apologies and recognitions of error that we noted earlier. In most cases, a person extending an apology ought to be forgiven. If the offense is constant and habitual, we can still forgive that person in our hearts without condoning their behavior. Even if the other party doesn't apologize, we shouldn't hold grudges or be unforgiving. In family relationships, many of us take these hard feelings to our graves.

Remember that it's the *intent* that's important. Stealing your property, defaming you, and taking credit for what you've accomplished are malicious. But taking the car when you didn't know I intended to use it and eating a snack that you were unaware I was saving for myself are not. We need to honestly confront the *motives* of the other person. If we extend grace and good will to other people, we will feel its reflected glow on ourselves.

---

[1] Marshall Goldsmith and Mark Reiter, *Triggers: Creating Behavior That Lasts— Becoming the Person You Want to Be* (New York: Crown Publishing, 2015).

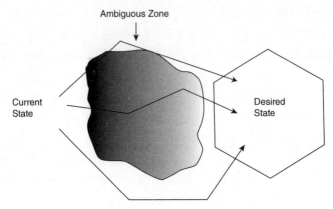

Figure 7.1   The Ambiguous Zone

Gaining and Sustaining Leverage

Leverage is power. Archimedes observed, "Give me a lever and I can move the world." Our plans are not so grand. We merely seek to move ourselves along in our journey.

For most people, leverage means moving on down the road expeditiously with minimal effort and friction. Journeys don't have to be difficult, and when they are it's usually because we've made them so by focusing on the unpleasant and unrewarding. Leverage helps us move by focusing on the positive and rewarding. Our experience with both organizational and individual change is *not* that people resist change—in fact, they usually highly desire the brighter future that's depicted. What they *do* often resist is the journey, because the journey is filled with ambiguity (darkness). These are roads not previously traveled.

So it's important to shed some light on the road.

As we can see from Figure 7.1, it takes longer to circumvent the ambiguous aspects of a journey. Shedding light on the paths available to us helps us take more direct routes. The question is how best to transit the ambiguous zone and to not be afraid of what might be in the dark.

When we encounter difficulties at the outset of a new venture, we have two options. One is to express our discontent, confusion, or uncertainties. There is a certain comfort in commiseration, as when many people are stranded by a storm together or frustrated by a new regulation that curtails their pleasure. However, too much commiseration creates a sense of victimhood and the covert or overt belief that the world is against you (see our earlier discussion about believing fatalistically that solely external forces control your life).

Another, healthier reaction to difficulties in your journey is being resolute: facing problems head on and solving as many of them as you can. In difficult situations, competence breeds confidence. People who tackle tough issues tend to have higher self-esteem, which results in increasing levels of competence: The better you feel about yourself, the more able and willing you are to solve problems, and the more you successfully solve problems the better you feel about yourself.

The idea is not to avoid the ambiguous zone nor to be hesitant about what may reside therein, but rather to boldly enter it knowing you have the skills and resources to effectively deal with whatever you find. Following are some techniques to improve your leverage.

Create Specific Goals

Although progress is a moving target, define your next mileposts in your journey. Don't allow an ambiguous zone to lead to an ambiguous future. Are you moving toward a degree, a new locality, an altered relationship, a change in health regimen, or travel to unfamiliar places? Whatever it is, be clear about the goal. For example, it's easier to accomplish planning a trip to London than it is to simply pursue "more international travel." It's far easier to achieve "better priority setting" than "being less overwhelmed."

Stay in the Moment

We tend to miss exits on the highway when we don't pay attention and to misread people and interactions when we're thinking about what to say next or trying too hard to please. While it's fine to keep your eye on distant targets, that shouldn't exclude understanding what's around you at present.

While we can look to the future with anticipation and learn from the past, the key trait lacking in many people is the ability to look at the present with acute awareness. Women tend to be better at this than men. There have been any number of times that I've left a meeting with one perception, only to have a female attendee point out cues in body language, the environment, and interactions that I missed.

Keep a Journal

We tend to write down what we have to do tomorrow, next week, and next month. We're not so good writing down what we've just done.

The importance of keeping a journal is that it hones our ability to reflect and learn from—and institutionalize—what we've done successfully. (I've always believed in post-celebrations and not post-mortems.) By keeping track, however briefly, of what's transpiring on our journey we can ensure that we create a success track that we can replay.

Milepost

It's better to know *why* we're good than *that* we're good.

Here's an example of a brief journal entry:

Date: March 3

Goal: Develop relationship with school board chair to explore becoming a member in the future.

Accomplishment: Set up appointment for Friday at 10 at her business office.

Insight: Accomplished this merely by calling and mentioning a mutual friend; there was no need for lengthy communications or a résumé. A personal referral is the fastest route.

Practice Conscious Positivity

The search for happiness, meaning, and general well-being is one of the major preoccupations of our society. In recent years an entirely new academic discipline—positive psychology—has emerged to explain and develop ideas about happiness, positivity, and well-being. At major universities, classes on the nature of happiness are among the most popular (and the professors who teach them are celebrities). Earlier I mentioned the work of Dan Gilbert at Harvard, who writes brilliantly about the nature of "synthetic" happiness. We can create happiness for ourselves, and the happiness we engineer through conscious effort is every bit as good as the happiness that lands in our laps felicitously and unexpectedly.

And yet there are those of us who still find it hard to be happy. In the developed world, we have more choice and material comfort than ever before in our lives, and yet depression rates continue to rise. Somehow, despite the abundance around us, we don't feel satisfied. Part of the reason is a feeling that we don't have control over our own lives. Earlier in this book, I (Marshall) mentioned my Daily Questions process, in which I'm asked a series of questions each day to keep my life on track. The way you phrase these questions is important. I have found that active questions are far more helpful than passive ones.

I learned about the power of active questions from my daughter, Dr. Kelly Goldsmith, who has a PhD from Yale University in behavioral marketing and teaches at Northwestern University's Kellogg School of Management.

Kelly and I are both fascinated with "employee engagement," the term used in management circles to describe a state of active involvement in work that you might liken to an athlete being in the zone. Kelly's key insight is this: If companies want their employees to be engaged, they should avoid handing out the typical surveys that ask workers what their bosses and managers can do to improve. These surveys aren't bad. They provide companies with many valuable suggestions. But they are diagnostic, not curative. They do nothing to put employees in engaged mind-sets.

Only employees themselves can do that—and a good way to remind them of this fact is to ask active questions about their working lives. For example, instead of asking the passive "Were you happy today?" (a question that invariably produces a laundry list of complaints), Kelly suggests asking the active question "Did you *do your best* to be happy today?" The ball is now in the employee's court. She has to make an evaluation and take responsibility for her own actions.

When we are active participants in our own engagement, happiness, or search for meaning in life, we gain a sense of control. We aren't waiting to see what the universe hands us. We know that whatever fate delivers, we have some agency—even if it's only in how we react.[2]

On our journey, we need to create our own happiness, our own engagement, our own joy, our own celebrations.

Recognize a Funny Thing

Humor has historically always reflected pain. The slapstick humor of slipping on a banana peel or the ironic humor of a stand-up comedian always reflects some inner angst or bad experience. Many people feel that most successful stand-ups are angry or had unhappy childhoods and are expressing their unhappiness in their observational humor.

Humor, especially when it's self-disparaging, can create great perspective. (Just recently I was massaging a finger I had to have operated on for a minor problem, per the surgeon's directions. While watching television, I was amazed at how much more flexible it had

---

[2] Marshall Goldsmith, *MOJO: How to Get It, How to Keep It, How to Get It Back If You Lose It* (New York: Hyperion, 2009).

become. When I looked down I realized I was massaging the wrong finger!)

How important is perspective on our journey? Here's comedian Louis C.K. on airline complaints: "You're complaining about comfort? You're sitting in a living room at 36,000 feet traveling at 500 miles an hour to get you to your destination in a fraction of the time it took before air travel. What are you complaining about?"

Now that we've embarked on our journey and have techniques to provide success, how do we sustain it so that it's a lifelong journey and not merely a day trip?

8 | Sustaining the Journey

Growth through Generosity

One of the more important elements in sealing watertight doors and sustaining our journey without sliding back is having a spirit of generosity. Being generous is about more than donating money, which is why we cite the spirit of generosity.

There was a successful entrepreneur who couldn't shake his scarcity mentality. At times, he was absolutely penurious, commenting that "Coach class arrives at the same time as first class, so why should I pay more?" I reminded him that paying more assured more comfort for himself and his family.

Similarly, he was very frugal with others. I told him that he had to have a more generous spirit. He reacted vehemently: "I *am* generous; look at what I've done for my family and myself!" I was too stunned to point out that generosity is an act of giving to others, not to yourself!

Many people are generous even as they themselves struggle. I remember my father putting an anonymous 10 dollars in someone's mailbox when he knew that person was struggling, despite the fact that 10 dollars was a lot of money back then and he was struggling to only a very slightly lesser degree himself.

I never forgot that example.

Conversely, some people remain ungenerous even after having reached high levels of success. While generosity is about more than just money, bear in mind that the idea of it is really based not so much on what you give *but rather what you have left after you give*. Hence, a billionaire donating $10,000 is far less impressive than someone who makes $50,000 donating $1,000.

The most precious gift is one of time and attention. Anyone can write a check. My son, an actor, was always more impressed by my wife and I attending off-off-Broadway, regional, and local theater productions than he was with the checks we wrote in support of these efforts. Time, after all, is a priority, not a resource. Since we know we have 24 hours every day—no matter who we are or at what level of success we are—how we distribute our time is vital. We are telling the world (and others) what our priorities are.

When a person says, "I'd love to watch my kid play soccer but I don't have the time," what they're really saying is, "I have other things I'm doing with my time." Those other things may be vital to earning money so that the kid can play soccer to begin with, but nonetheless, *it's a decision we make based on our priorities at the time.*

Hence, donating our time is a huge act of generosity, whether by volunteering, serving on committees, coaching, or by whatever other means. It's easy to be generous by changing our priorities about how we spend our time.

What can you be generous about? Surprisingly, perhaps, a great many things in addition to time, such as:

- *Money:* Most nonprofits and charities receive most of their money from a high volume of small donations, not from large ones. (Crowdsourcing has been tremendously effective, from funding political campaigns to helping launch start-ups.) Don't think you have to be a huge donor to have an impact on a cause. Providing $100 can be substantial. Providing $25, or even $5, can make an impact if the donor pool is large enough. And don't limit your contributions to well-known causes. It's easy to go to your town's welfare or human services department, ask if they have provision for helping those in need, and make an anonymous donation. Most religious institutions provide a vehicle for these donations and you don't have to be a member to make one.

- *Services:* Your in-kind contributions can make a difference. You can provide advice, food, advertising, marketing, physical property, transportation, and an array of other products and services to organizations that need them. Some of my coaching clients are executive recruiters who offer to help find staff and volunteer talent *pro bono*.

- *Repute:* If you serve on a committee, or make calls on the phone, or sign an email, your status in the community can help influence others to join or contribute to the cause. There are people who know you, people who know of you, and people who are justifiably impressed when there's a long list of supporters behind an initiative with your name lending heft to that list.

Digression

There are members of my coaching community who specialize in "return on philanthropy." This means that when donations and support are intelligently managed, there is a commensurate improvement in brand, repute, visibility, and business. I'm not advocating a give-to-get mentality, but my experience (and these people's businesses) validate that generosity is often directly rewarded—even when you're not seeking that direct reward.

- *Support and comfort:* One of the greatest kinds of generosity is simply listening and supporting. The circumstances may be dire—a grave illness or the loss of a loved one—or temporary—the loss of a job, a broken relationship, or a great disappointment. Whatever the issue, the gesture of simply listening and not judging, of supporting and not evaluating, is a huge act of generosity, demonstrating that it's for the other person and not yourself. There's a huge difference among these three responses, for example:

1. "How on earth could you have done that? I don't blame you for feeling awful."
2. "You were wrong, here's how I would have handled it and how you can handle it next time."
3. "Tell me about it. What are your feelings right now?"

Case Study

My son was expecting the lead role in a production of *The Grapes of Wrath* during his senior year majoring in drama in the theater school at the University of Miami. Unexpectedly, and without precedent, the department brought in an outsider for the role. My son was distraught and called me.

"I feel dreadful," he said, "betrayed, disappointed, shocked, and saddened."

"How can I help?" I asked.

"Tell me how I should feel," he said.

"You should feel exactly as you do. That's how I'd feel in the same circumstances."

"Really?!"

"Yes, your feelings are understandable, appropriate, and legitimate. *But the question now is what you do about them.* You can protest to the dean, refuse to perform in the play, tell others not to attend—or you can accept another role and do the best possible job you can."

He took another role and was terrific, and he learned a great lesson. I learned that it's important to validate someone else's feelings without judging him.

And we all have to realize that it's not what happens to us in life that matters so much as what we decide to do about it. (There's that issue of internal versus external control once again.)

Let's conclude this discussion by emphasizing the need for *a generosity of spirit*. It's defined as the intent of giving without the expectation of receiving. It may mean treating someone not as you would expect to be treated but rather *as she would prefer to be treated*. Nontangible, ineffable acts of generosity are highly effective.

It's easy to write a check, but it's harder (and highly effective) to patiently listen. If you're waiting for someone to wave a thank you at you after you've paused to let him turn in front of you on the road, and you're ticked off when he doesn't, that's not generosity. That's self-absorption.

I (Marshall) believe that you get more when you give more.

Our values are key to designing our lives, to becoming the people we want to be, to creating the lives we want. If we live our values, it shows. For instance, my values are generosity and teaching. So I give all of my material away on my website. You can copy, share, download, and duplicate it. It's all free. In return for giving, I get more wonderful people in my life, and more amazing experiences—more than I ever could have imagined. Counterintuitive, yes—and absolutely true in my experience.

When I was young, there was a program in Kentucky, where I grew up, called the March of Dimes Bread Drive. My high school was one of the poorer schools in the area, and I was put in charge of the bread drive for my area.

We were instructed to knock on doors in our neighborhood. When someone answered the door, we were to ask that person, "Would you make a donation?" If the person made a donation, then we were to give her a loaf of bread.

I told my team, "We're going to do something different. We're going to give them the bread. Then we'll tell them, 'If you want or are able to make a donation that would be nice, if not that's okay too. Either way, we're going to give you the loaf of bread.'"

You see, to me, it was demeaning to try to bribe people with a loaf of bread. If they can give you something back for it, great. But maybe they can't right then, maybe they can't afford it, maybe they aren't capable of it. That's okay too.

It was during that March of Dimes Bread Drive that I really started to live the philosophy of giving. It's been a good life philosophy for me to just "give people the bread." And in Valley Station, Kentucky, those many years ago, my little March of Dimes Bread Drive team ended up raising more money than any other team in the county!

Today I'm giving the bread away again with my legacy project, 100 Coaches. I am very honored to have this opportunity to once again give away the bread!

Evolution through Exploration

When Cortés landed in the New World, he was concerned that his men would be frightened and would desert. So he burned the ships on which they had sailed. Without another option, they were better off sticking together and following their leader.

What Cortés did after that in subduing the Aztecs is repugnant to many. But we're focused here only on the efficacy of destroying the means of retreat. (As noted previously, the Aztecs had their own version of preventing retreat: an ankle staked to the ground.) In other words, what are the parallels here for shutting the watertight doors firmly and moving forward, not back?

We've all seen crabs, rabbits, spiders, and all sorts of creatures that retreat into a burrow or nook when scared. People create these burrows, too, and sometimes rarely emerge because venturing outside is considered too risky.

Yet our journey demands exploration. The road that others used may not be our road. It's not a question of the road more traveled or less traveled, but perhaps of building our own road where none has existed. This demands some prudent poking about, looking around the next corner, shining lights in the darkness, and feeling our way.

To explore, you can't merely *think* outside the box. You have to *be* outside the box. Some examples:

- A woman in the marketing business also happened to be a superb classical pianist. She had never thought the two talents could be combined, but advice to use her music in her work led to metaphors about harmony and innovation, as well as her own music accompanying some of her promotional material and collateral. She achieved a powerful, highly rewarding synergy between avocation and occupation.[1]

- For many years I've heard from Canadian consultants that it's too hard to work in the United States—too much paperwork and hassle crossing the border (yet I've worked in Canada as a consultant for 30 years). A woman from Ottawa, who's become a thought leader in sales strategies, figured out how to easily live for six months in Canada and six months in Florida, and developed a thriving seven-figure practice in doing what is a hassle to others.

We have to think differently and think *bigger*. Instead of extrapolating from where we are today and looking at arithmetic growth, we must paint a picture of the future and decide how to achieve it through geometric growth. Our journey is a moving target. We create our future (internal control) and intelligently manage the world around us (external control) as we progress. What we can't do is allow external control to determine our future.

Case Study

I (Alan) first encountered one of the newer, whooshing machines that rapidly dry your hands in an airport restroom. I decided it was brilliant. Unlike older, slower models, it dried your hands completely, was sanitary, and required no messy paper towels.

When I looked to see who had manufactured it, I was stunned to see that it was Dyson, a company that I had always regarded as a

[1] One of my favorite stories is about her stopping to play one of the ubiquitous pianos in a Ritz-Carlton hotel. A security guy came over and told her that she couldn't play the piano. "Apparently, I can," she replied, continuing with her music.

vacuum cleaner manufacturer (with great television commercials). Then it came to me: Dyson wasn't in the vacuum cleaner business, it was *in the air movement business.*

Dyson was thinking much bigger than their current and original products. It was thinking about what processes and expertise were driving the business and could be exploited in other ways. I'm waiting for the Dyson hair dryer.

Imagine if IBM (International Business Machines, literally) believed that it was only in the computer punch card and machine business instead of the information technology business?

Exploration requires that we abandon notions of what we can and cannot do. We're all pleasantly surprised when someone introduces us to something we're sure we'll be poor at (or dislike— often *because* we're sure we'll be poor at it) and our performance is pretty good! That applies to skills, talents, tastes, and all kinds of experiences. It's fine to say you don't like a certain food's taste, *but not if you've never tasted it.* Okay, it may be one thing to turn down fish eyeballs (a delicacy in some parts of Asia) but it's quite another to say, "I'm sure I wouldn't like lobster."

How many of these areas have you actively denied yourself the experience of trying?

- Playing a musical instrument
- Ballroom dancing
- Participative sports
- Hiking and backpacking
- Foreign travel
- Individual water and snow sports
- Live theater
- Volunteering on holidays
- Singing
- Painting and photography

One of the reasons we're dissuaded is that many people who are involved in these pursuits are quite serious and have become experts of one sort or another. They intimidate us: "Her voice is beautiful; I could never do that." "He has his own scuba gear." "She's hiked the Appalachian Trail." "He's flown gliders."

None of that eliminates the opportunity to simply enjoy ourselves as we explore new outlets for our talents, and that opportunity is the key: Exploration is about allowing our talents to blossom, to be recognized, to be further developed, to be shared with others.

Over the past decade we've noticed that the most effective motivators in the business world are not money or status. They are opportunities to be autonomous, to apply one's talents, and to be recognized for the successful application of those talents. Exactly the same dynamic applies to all of us in our individual journeys.

But talents need outlets, and we need to be outside the box. Some years ago we met an American couple while traveling in Japan. The woman always chose a restaurant where she could order pasta. Her husband told us that this was her favorite dish, and the only one she would eat, no matter where she was! (You can't make this stuff up!) That's not exactly exploration, even if you have traveled 8,000 miles.

Exploration involves risk (which for some people draws them to it mightily). More obvious risks are seen in exploring caves, climbing mountains, scuba diving, and learning to fly. But there are other risks beyond obvious physical ones. Many of us find great risk in public speaking, or in exhibiting something we've created, or in expressing our opinions to others, or in trying a new food!

These risks emerge from fear of rejection and fear of damaging our egos—fear of perceived failure. Yet no journey is flawless. There will be risks that need to be accepted and undertaken.

Here's a brief examination of risk, a pragmatic view of what we're really talking about, which may induce you to be more of a prudent risk taker. While we're not advocating a trip to the poker table, we do endorse a more insightful understanding of your own (internal) control of risk.

There are two basic components to risk assessment:

1. *Probability:* What is the likelihood of an adverse event or condition occurring?
2. *Seriousness:* What is the extent of the adverse impact if it does
   occur?

For example, the probability of an airplane crash is extraordinarily
low, but the seriousness is huge. The probability of my slipping and
falling on an icy sidewalk in the winter is very high (in my experience)
but the seriousness is quite low (embarrassment, no physical harm).

We can mitigate probability risk through *preventive action*. Planes
are strictly serviced and reengineered and examined. You see pilots
going through physical examinations and checklists before every
flight. I can hold on to something while walking on icy pavement,
or can find another route, or can use footwear that is safer on such
surfaces.

We can also reduce the seriousness of an event should it occur.
Aircraft have emergency exits, oxygen masks, and life jackets. Airports
have emergency vehicles on standby. I can wear padded clothing to
cushion a fall and put ice or heat on bruises or injuries.

In your home and place of work, you have fire extinguishers,
sprinkler systems, and emergency exits to mitigate the risk from fire.
But you also have No Smoking signs, isolation of combustibles, and
certain standards for electrical wiring to *prevent* fires. Think of risk
mitigation as "prevent and protect."

Therefore, take preventive and contingent (protective) actions to
help you safely on your journey. You can't eliminate all risk, nor should
you attempt to (or you'd never leave the house, let alone embark on
a life's journey). But you can effectively manage risk yourself.

As you can see in Figure 8.1, you can correct and/or adapt to
events that have already occurred, and can prevent or protect yourself from risks in the future. (Insurance policies are comforting, but
don't overlook the fact that the adverse event has already transpired
for insurance to be a mitigating option.)

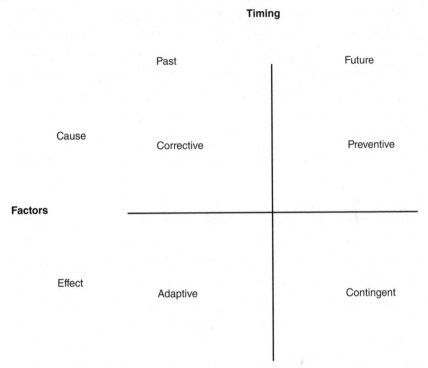

Timing

Past   Future

Cause
          Corrective   Preventive

Factors

Effect
          Adaptive   Contingent

Figure 8.1   The Types of Actions Available

Your exploration to sustain your journey needn't be dangerous, even if it's not without some natural risk.

New Dimensions of Relationships

Some relationships are permanent; examples can include our families, life partners, close friends, and professional colleagues. Of course, we may be alienated from some family members, and divorce among married couples is not rare. Close friends may move, or we may move, both physically and philosophically. But we do, nevertheless, usually form lifelong bonds with some people.

These venerable relationships endure not necessarily because of frequency of contact. We may see some family members only on holidays and keep in touch with certain friends from a distance through the phone and email. Even in marriages and partnerships there can be separations caused by job demands, military service, and family emergencies. Many people claim that a business partnership can be more demanding than a marriage, and that a breakup between business partners is tougher than any divorce.

These days we probably have an easier time than ever before maintaining friendships, since we can Skype, Zoom, email, call from cell phones, text, Instagram, and use a variety of social media platforms. More on these in a moment.

Other relationships are transient. These are friends, acquaintances, coworkers, and colleagues who enter and leave our lives as we enter and leave theirs. Parting can be voluntary or involuntary. Such relationships can be highly valuable and rewarding, even if only for the short term. We've all had the experience—in going through school or serving in the military or taking on a temporary work assignment or even taking a vacation—of enjoying the company of people we've been associated with temporarily, even if we didn't continue the relationship beyond the vacation, assignment, tour of duty, or whatever brought us together.

Transient relationships can last for a few days or a few years. They can be highly enriching or quickly forgotten. I'm sure you've had the experience of finding your seatmate on an airplane to be absolutely fascinating—or deadly boring! In the first case you're sorry when the flight has to end, as you both rush off to the next stage of your travels; in the latter you wish that you could hide out in the restroom.

Still other relationships are virtual, which is a type that's quite new, relatively speaking. We spoke earlier about the use of technology to stay in touch with permanent and transient relationships, but here we're talking about the nature of the relationship itself. We form connections (note that they're called "followers" or "friends" or, literally, "connections") with electronic representations of people. We may see their photos and be able to read their words, but we don't interact in the classic sense. There is no body language, inflection, intonation, volume, pitch, nonverbal behavior, or gesticulation.

Electronic media and social platforms are flat. They have no depth. (This is why, in business relationships, personal meetings are best, followed by video chat and videoconferencing technology, followed by phone, followed last by email.) Social media does a lot of good in connecting people, empowering movements, and boosting worthy causes. But it presents challenges, too. We can see and experience language and reactions on social media that would never occur in person, such as trolls who attack others for no reason, gratuitous use of obscenity, polarizing opinions, name calling, and so forth. A flat medium permits that. Such behavior, if manifested in a face-to-face, public setting would be considered gross and coarse. People make political, sexual, and religious comments on social media that they would never utter in the actual presence of other people.[2]

Consequently, our third dimension of relationships—virtual—requires discretion for these reasons:

- Nothing published on any social media platform, no matter how restrictive you are in setting your connection permissions, is ever private or actually restricted to that platform. There is a good chance that clients will learn of your private views.
- There are attack dogs on social media platforms who are always on the prowl spoiling for a fight. Many of them are bullies with vast inferiority complexes (the hallmark of bullies) who are seeking to bring everyone down to their own levels of poor self-worth. Such fights can be enervating. You need to ruthlessly cull your virtual connections for this reason.
- Social media platforms can turn into vast vanity publishing operations, allowing anyone to say almost anything. And what is said becomes indelible. We all leave a trail. It's hard to erase things that have been posted in the past unless you delete your

---

[2] YouTube is probably the largest of the social media platforms; it has somewhat more depth because it is visual, but it is also one of the sites with the most obscene and profane communications.

account entirely. What you've published two years ago can return to haunt you next year.

Virtual friends may, indeed, be either transient or permanent relationships—and, as we stated, many permanent and transient relationships are enhanced by the use of social media. But there is a difference between the use of social media as a communications tool for face-to-face relationships *versus a source for developing new relationships.*

With those distinctions in mind, let's now focus on sustaining your journey through relationships, whether permanent or temporary or virtual, with these four goals in mind:

1. *We have to give to get.* For relationships to be fulfilling we have to invest in them; we can't simply be takers. What we offer needn't be tangible (although it could be), but can be in the form of listening, support, feedback, commiseration, and empathy. Relationships are two-way, reciprocal streets. You can't hog the road.

2. *Relationships are based on trust.* Trust is the honest-to-God belief that the other person has your best interests in mind and that you have her best interests in mind. Therefore, feedback and advice, however painful, are part of the tough love of actually caring for the other party—so much so that you must be painfully honest when it's called for. (We've found too many businesses that don't trust their own customers, creating truly lousy and unproductive customer relationships.)

3. *Relationships are not a zero-sum game.* For me to win, you don't have to lose. For you to win, I don't have to lose. We can both win (or lose). *I am not diminished by your victories.* We have to rejoice in success and bemoan loss for either party.

4. *Relationships need to be appropriate.* If you're promoted, your former colleagues are now subordinates, and your former superiors are now peers. When you move into a new neighborhood, your new relationships will tend to be different from your prior

ones. You can reach a level of familiarity and ease in a personal relationship that may not be right for a professional relationship. Similarly, social relationships have their own unspoken rules. You wouldn't act the same way—I wouldn't think—with your golfing buddy as you would with your prospective father-in-law.

Relationships fuel your journey. Some are constant sources of power, some are present for certain intervals and provide guidance and help. There are others, however, which should be avoided, ended, or minimized because they represent unwanted detours, excess weight, or distraction.

Legacy

Let me (Marshall) take you on an imaginary journey into the future. I want you to imagine that you're 95 years old and you're lying on your deathbed. Just before you take your last breath, you're given a wonderful gift—the ability to go back in time and visit yourself as you are now. What advice would the wise 95-year-old you, who has lived a long life and knows what really matters, have for your current self? Would the problems that consume you seem big or small? Would you put off your own happiness, or would you claim it in the present moment, knowing that you don't really have all that many moments left? Earlier I shared with you my philosophy that you should be happy now, not later, not after you've achieved something or earned a certain amount of money. Let me add to that: If you have a dream, go for it now. It's not going to get easier to follow your dreams when you're older. The dream doesn't have to be big. It can be anything: learning to knit, hiking the Appalachian Trail, having children, or playing the guitar. Don't pay any attention to what other people think about it. This is your life, your dream, and your chance to be happy. When you get old, it will be your legacy.

Legacy is often thought of as something left behind or handed down by a predecessor. While that may be true and common—her legacy in medicine is a benefit to us all—what's not so commonly understood is that legacies do not appear upon retirement, departure, or death.

Legacies are created daily.

Every day you're writing the story of your life—another page, another chapter. Your legacy is on those pages. The question is, of course: Are others going to read a boring book where each page is basically identical to the one preceding it, or will they read a splendid story that evolves and contains surprises and leaves a strong message for the reader? And perhaps even a philosophy, a set of skills, or a value system?

Two thousand years after they wrote we still read Homer, Socrates, and Aristotle. Global religions were begun by individuals thousands of years ago. The plays of Shakespeare and Molière still delight us, as do the stories of Dickens and Chekhov. Louis Armstrong, Billie Holiday, and Frank Sinatra have left legacies with their music. Madame Curie, Jonas Salk, and Alexander Fleming created legacies in medicine.

But closer to home, more intimately, we are the beneficiaries of legacies within our families, our communities, our professions. One of my uncles left me the legacy of laughter. A business owner for whom I worked left me the legacy of entrepreneurialism. Many people have provided me with the legacy of community service and philanthropy.

What we're telling you may be somewhat shocking at first: You can consciously create your legacy, *starting now*. Too many people are unaware of this opportunity or ignore it, at their peril. Think about it: If you are consciously thinking about *contribution* and what you provide for others, not just for your lifetime but for theirs, might that not color and influence your behaviors and decisions today?

Here are three actual examples of our acknowledging this phenomenon in our lives and work:

1. *The* Wall Street Journal *test:* Business leaders are often asked, "Would you feel good if that decision or action were on the

front page of the *Wall Street Journal* tomorrow morning?" That is, is a decision or action the kind of example and representation of you and your company that you want others to know about? Would others be proud and want to emulate it, or would they cringe and seek to avoid you?

2. *The Kantian categorical imperative:* With respect ethics and proper behavior, Kant asked, essentially, "What if everyone did that?" When people believe that no harm is done, or that they can get away with something not entirely proper (or ethical or even legal), what would be the result if everyone thought that way? (If you cut a line yourself, you might get a few harsh comments, but if everyone sought to do it there would be anarchy and injury.)

3. *Is that the lesson you want to teach your kids?* Granted, not everyone has children, but the same principle applies to any member of the youngest generation. We are often asked, "Is this the model I want my children (or children in general) to follow?" Do I want them to treat all people well or to be prejudiced? Do I prefer that they study hard or try to cheat? We do modify our behaviors based on who's impressionable and watching.

Digression

The greatest legacy we leave in many cases is our children, not merely in terms of their existence but with respect to their values and subsequent behaviors. Nurturing and home environment are two basic and powerful determinants of adult behavior (along with societal norms and pressures). We hear our kids say all the time, "When did I become my mother?" or "OMG, I'm acting like my father!"

If for no other reason than the ever-observing children, we need to think carefully about legacy, not in terms of some distant bequest, but rather in daily terms of lessons and morality.

The family dinner has all but disappeared. Extracurricular activities, dual-working parents, electronic games and diversions, sports, and a myriad of other distractions have ended nightly discussions over a meal. We were poor, but I nonetheless listened to my parents try to decide how to pay the bills, whether or not to seek new work, and how to handle difficult family members. I was also able to hear from them about my school challenges, other kids cheating in class, and unfair treatment.

The individual role models we provide are more crucial and far reaching than ever before.

Thus, we do have to acknowledge that there is a need to create models and examples, avatars of conduct. That's what we mean by legacy being written every day and not simply at the end of one's life or involvement with others.

The decisions and behaviors you choose to engage in every day are the woof and warp of your legacy. Just as there are athletes, entertainers, politicians, researchers, business leaders, and others whose legacy we can appreciate daily, there are people in our lives doing the same thing, though we may not realize it as such. Consequently, we are (or are not) providing similar episodes in our legacy daily for others around us.

If history holds true, some of you reading this book will contact us and let us know of the change it made in your lives. Some of you will recommend it to others. We write our books with that clearly in mind. We don't recommend fads, or simply emulate others' works, or experiment in our pages. Our responsibility is to help you to improve your lives by carefully adding to our own legacy.

That's not selfish, that's a contribution!

What contributions are you making? The Kantian categorical imperative applies to positive behaviors as well. We've witnessed pay-it-forward and gift-it-forward movements on social media, as well as viral appeals for charitable giving (e.g., the ice bucket challenge). What if everyone did what you did in terms of being generous, providing help, donating time and money, spending time with your family, admitting mistakes and apologizing, maintaining your health?

In Japanese society, there is chaos in the subways, with professional pushers helping to pack the cars inhumanly full. Yet on their bullet trains, the cars stop perfectly at particular spots on the platform and people board in an orderly fashion with no problem or inconvenience. Even within one culture, we can find significant examples of differences in conduct.

So we ask you here perhaps the most important question in the book: What are you doing now, today, to build your legacy while on your evolutionary journey? It will seldom be one grand gesture, and will more probably be a continuing series of positive actions that not only help you and help others but provide a lasting guide for others to use along their own journeys.

Lifestorming is about taking on life and enjoying it immensely by contributing to it enormously. We hope we've enhanced your journey by sharing lessons of our own.

9

Self-Mastery: The *Lifestorming* Field Guide to Your Successful Journey

Over decades of coaching others, we've found that there is a discernible, practical difference between those who make little headway after learning new techniques and those who absolutely rocket forward past others, having found new fuel and vigor. We've included this chapter as our admonition to be among the latter, including our best practices as to how to do it.

If you truly wish to apply our principles of Lifestorming to your own journey—and you're on a journey whether or not you've acknowledged it, despite its direction, speed, or progress—then these are the distinguishing features of those who are most successful in that pursuit.

1. *Apply the learning immediately, right now, without any waiting.* You can't wait for "the right time" or "the proper situation." You must proactively *seek* an immediate use. For example, if you wish to focus on building aspects of character, choose the trait most important and find resources to help you improve right now. If you want to examine the relevance of your beliefs and values, write them down and ask if

they represent your current thinking. If you want to change and/or enlarge friendships, describe the people you'd like to have for friends and find a way to meet them.

2. *Share your intent.* An important aspect of creating accountability is to include others in your plans so that they can inquire about progress (as well as help you with it). We mentioned earlier that people who have overweight waiters tend to order more food, and those who watch others exercise tend to exercise harder themselves. Find people who have made significant changes, who are on their own journeys, and become accountable to them as well.

3. *Pursue success, not perfection.* Don't allow a setback to overturn the entire cart. Not everything will work perfectly, you'll have some non-success, and you'll get frustrated ("I'm still self-editing too much."). That's okay. Acknowledge now that the journey has obstacles and can be slower going at times; just don't allow them to lead you to the off ramp. Be resilient, and use setbacks as learning opportunities that support future successes.

4. *Journal and record.* In the mornings, take a minute to tell yourself what you're going to accomplish, and in the evenings tell yourself what you have accomplished. Use a hard copy, electronic, or audio journal to record your thoughts and observations. Talking through your experiences helps you to better understand those experiences. Focus on the positive and continually strive to find the positive in every day's experiences.

5. *Focus and build on strengths.* As you realize the greatest progress, find the causes and replicate them. You'll make much faster progress building on strengths than you will trying to correct perceived weaknesses. If you find that assuming leadership roles is working well for you, then take on another one or expand the ones you have. This will provide momentum for improvement in other areas as well.

6. *Make changes consistent with your direction and progress.* We've discussed lifelong friends, transient friends, and new friends—make changes here consistent with your journey's direction. Your relationships, whether intimate or merely casual, should be consistent with your goals and not antithetical to them. The same would be true of your interests, hobbies, memberships, and so forth.

7. *Your journey is both strategic and tactical.* Your direction—who you want to become, and the nature and direction of your life—is the strategic nature of your journey. Your decisions on the journey about the factors and challenges we've discussed throughout the book are tactical. Thus, your daily decisions are to execute your overarching strategy. Your decisions on the road have to be in support of the destination you've chosen, not the other way around.

8. *Ask "What's in it for me?"* It's fine—in fact, vital—to be "healthily selfish." You won't make progress on your journey by consistently sacrificing for others. Counterintuitively, you can best help others by helping yourself. The better you feel about yourself the more confident you'll be. Once you achieve that state you can intelligently help others in win/win and not win/lose relationships. If you keep moving over for others you'll forever be in the slow lane on your journey.

9. *Keep raising the bar.* This is a *journey*, not an event. As you make progress and become more successful, the bar should be raised, and you're the one to raise it. Don't be content with beating the same standard over and over—that's not how world records are set. Keep raising the bar. The current high-jump and pole-vault heights were unthinkable 10 years ago, as are the ones that will exist 10 years from now.

10. *Understand at all times that what is today is not what is.* We often fall in to the trap of thinking that today is the be-all and end-all of life. It is not; it's simply another way station along the journey. A patent official infamously announced in the late nineteenth century that the patent office ought to be closed because everything that could be invented had been invented. What's new today will be old tomorrow. The only constant is change.

Testing Yourself

Here are our questions for you to ask yourself to create self-mastery, following the chronology of the book. We suggest you insert them into your daily calendar and ask yourself on a daily basis about your progress (or lack thereof). These would also provide a fine structure to any journaling you choose to do per our advice above. They are keyed to each chapter, and may be used after reading the book as a "field guide" and/or while reading the book as an aid in immediate application.

Chapter 1: Misguided Aspirations

Why we tend to create the wrong goals and the wrong metrics

1. What have I been told I should be or become?

   _____

2. Who do I *really* wish to become?

   _____

   _____

3. What is the actual internal control (shown in Figure 9.1) that I can exert daily for myself?

   _____

   _____

4. Here's a brief test on your personal metrics and norms:
   I. Choose someone you consider to be a personal hero. It could be someone from a life experience, such as a teacher, or

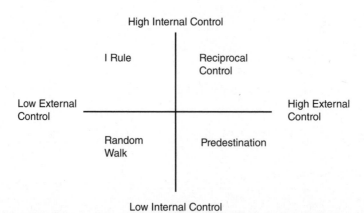

Figure 9.1   Internal versus External Control

someone in the news, such as Sully Sullenberger (who landed his powerless plane in the Hudson with no loss of life):

_____

II. Write the personal traits of that person, as you define them, on the lines below. Try to think of at least seven. These could be patience, or boldness, or great use of language, and so forth:

1. _____

2. _____

3. _____

4. _____

5. _____

6. _____

7. _____

III. Now, return to the top, cross off your hero's name, and write yours in.

IV. List below which of these traits you already possess and which must be developed:

A. __ Possess
   __ Need to develop: _____
B. __ Possess
   __ Need to develop: _____
C. __ Possess
   __ Need to develop: _____
D. __ Possess
   __ Need to develop: _____
E. __ Possess
   __ Need to develop: _____

     F. __ Possess
       __ Need to develop: _____

    G. __ Possess
       __ Need to develop: _____

5. What can you extricate yourself from that today captures you in a frenetic "spinning wheel" of activity but not fulfillment (e.g., social media)?

_____

_____

6. What detours threaten your journey, and how can you ignore or bypass them?

_____

_____

7. What are your major sources for standards, beliefs, and aspirations?

_____

_____

2. The Mythology of Friends for Life

The impermanence of permanence

8. What normative pressures do you feel the most?

_____

_____

9. What can you do to change or eliminate them?

_____

_____

10. Who are your valued, lifelong friends?

_____

_____

11. Are there friends who have become negative and dysfunctional? Who are they?

_____

_____

12. What friends, by name or by type, would you like to acquire during your journey?

_____

_____

13. Whom do you live through (if anyone) vicariously?

_____

_____

14. What level are you on among the watertight doors (shown in Figure 9.2)?

_____

_____

15. What can you do to attain the next level and/or firmly seal the doors behind you?

_____

_____

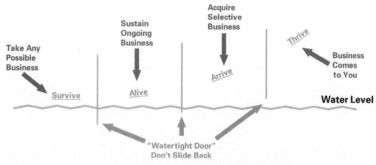

Figure 9.2   Watertight Doors

16. What do you most have to let go of in order to reach out in bolder and more satisfying ways?

_____

_____

17. What do you need to more broadly generalize and give yourself credit for instead of calling your accomplishment "luck" or a one-time success?

_____

_____

18. What is your most serious example of scarcity thinking or poverty mentality and how will you change it?

_____

_____

19. Where are you on the self-esteem chart (see Figure 9.3), and how will you migrate to the upper left and/or sustain yourself in the upper left?

_____

_____

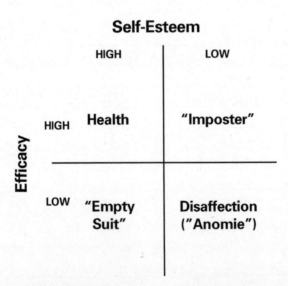

Figure 9.3   Esteem and Abundance

Behavioral Metamorphosis

If you're not careful, the butterfly may be no more beautiful than the caterpillar

20. What usually takes more time or money than you originally estimated?

_____

_____

What's the main reason for your answers?

_____

_____

21. When and why have you been successful in stopping bad habits cold turkey without requiring help?

_____

22. What behaviors do you seek to change?

_____

_____

23. What behaviors will you substitute?

_____

_____

24. What assistance will you need?

_____

_____

25. What metrics will show that you're making progress?

_____

_____

26. What will you do to sustain the change?

_____

_____

27. What beliefs do you currently hold that ought to be examined for their validity in shaping your attitudes and behavior?

_____

_____

28. What is your immediate reaction to unpleasant news or poor behavior on someone else's part?

    _____

    _____

29. Would you make any changes to these immediate reactions and in what way?

    _____

    _____

30. How much permission do you usually allow yourself (see Figure 9.4)?

    _____

    _____

31. How can you best improve and sustain the proper permissions as you improve your behaviors and continue on your journey?

    _____

    _____

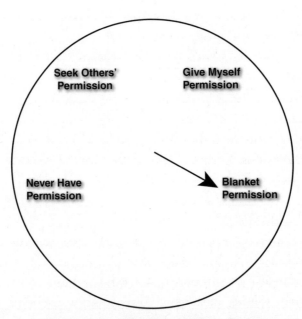

Figure 9.4 The Permission Gauge

4. Believe It or Not

Do you believe me or your lying eyes?

32. When and where, if ever, do you feel like a fraud or imposter and why?

   _____

   _____

33. Are you fearful of being arrogant or called arrogant? On what occasions?

   _____

   _____

34. How would you describe the "real you"?

   _____

   _____

35. What do you think "authenticity" means for you?

   _____

   _____

36. What are your basic beliefs about yourself, for example, what you are great at (teaching), what you just can't do (play an instrument), how you respond (impatient), and so forth?

   _____

   _____

37. What merits reconsideration and/or change (you could take piano lessons, learn to swim better, leave your corporate job and start your own business)?

   _____

   _____

38. What actions and behaviors should be modified, created, or abandoned in light of those changes (resign from a group, confront a poor relationship, make different investments)?

   _____

   _____

39. Do you tend to use purely logic, purely emotion, or a combination of both in major decisions?

_____

_____

40. What's one obviously false belief you've held onto for too long?

_____

_____

5. The Importance and Evolution of Character

Understanding and improving the essential nature of exactly who you are

41. For our character test, rate yourself on a 1-to-5 scale on our elements:
    1. Can't really justify that this is at all like me.
    2. Occasionally, I could be described this way.
    3. In some circumstances, I'm always like this.
    4. I'm usually in this description.
    5. I'm constantly like this.

    Score

Intelligence	_____
Drive	_____
Happiness	_____
Empathy	_____
Reciprocity	_____
Intimacy	_____

42. Is there an example of a critical ethical decision you had to make and, if so, are you happy with the outcome?

_____

_____

43. Where would you place yourself on the happiness/meaning evaluation (shown in Figure 9.5)?

_____

_____

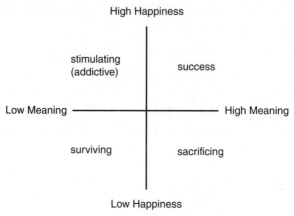

Figure 9.5   Happiness and Meaning

44. What would you consider your usual esteem level to be?

_____

_____

45. How well do you do creating consistency in turbulent times?

_____

_____

46. How often do you serve in the role of informal leader?

_____

_____

47. Do you know when to apologize and do you do so effectively and calmly?

_____

_____

48. To what extent are you sharing credit and accepting blame? In what areas can you share credit in the future on a consistent basis?

_____

_____

49. Do you make tough decisions or do you procrastinate or ask someone else to make them?

_____

_____

50. What tough decisions do you see on the horizon, and how will you prepare for them?

_____

_____

51. Rate yourself on a scale of 1 (I need improvement), 2 (I'm good but not consistent), or 3 (I'm continually excellent), then add your score:
    - Meeting deadlines
    - Fulfilling your commitments
    - Completing tasks rapidly
    - Locating information needed quickly
    - Planning your time
    - Establishing correct priorities
    - Assessing risk and reward potential
    - Identifying and mobilizing resources
    - Building teams appropriate to the tasks
    - Making rapid, successful decisions
    - Solving problems rapidly and correctly
    - Creating new ideas and innovating

6. Critical Abandonment

Knowing when to hold and when to fold

52. What business or personal relationships should be abandoned or reduced?

_____

_____

53. What is your home base for change? (See Figure 9.6.)

_____

_____

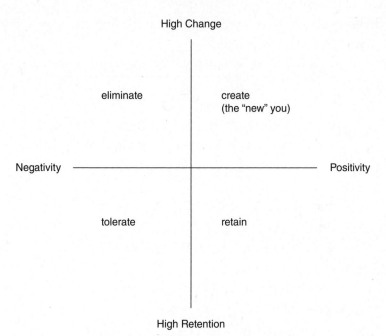

Figure 9.6   Critical Abandonment

54. Think of two people in your life or who should be in your life (in the case of "create") who fill these roles:

_____

_____

Eliminate:

1. _____
2. _____

Accept:

1. _____
2. _____

Preserve:

1. _____
2. _____

Create:

1. _____
2. _____

Now answer this: What action is required for each?

Actions

Eliminate:

1. _____
2. _____

Accept:

1. _____
2. _____

Preserve:

1. _____
2. _____

Create:

1. _____
2. _____

55. What, if any, organizations and memberships should you walk away from that don't fit or support your journey?

_____

_____

56. What life do I envision for myself a year from now?

_____

_____

57. If I had the chance, who would I like to meet and develop a relationship with?

_____

_____

58. What am I accepting as a "necessary evil" or as an obligation I impose on myself?

_____

_____

59. Am I using personal metrics for progress and success, or someone else's?

_____

_____

60. Which of my quadrants is most heavily weighted at the moment, and how can I put more emphasis on creating?

_____

_____

61. If I look back a year, have I made the progress I had anticipated?

_____

_____

62. Currently on your journey, which position shown in Figure 9.7 are you in?

_____

63. What do you need to do to reach position #4 in Figure 9.7 *and sustain it?*

_____

_____

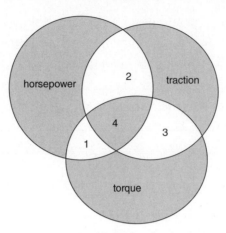

Figure 9.7   The Vehicle on the Journey

64. Where is your current growth on the axes shown in Figure 9.8 and what is your priority area for further growth? What actions will you take?

_____

_____

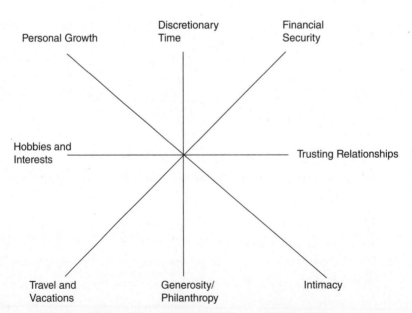

Figure 9.8   Personal Growth Metrics

7. *The New You*

Shedding the old baggage and creating new norms and capabilities

65. What causes you the most fear and why?

_____

_____

66. How can you get rid of it?

_____

_____

67. Under what conditions have you ever choked or panicked? Do you feel you've overcome the reaction under those conditions?

_____

_____

68. How can you improve your visualization of future events that are now somewhat unfamiliar to you?

_____

_____

69. What situations or interpersonal situations make you feel guilty?

_____

_____

70. Who are the people who most attempt to make you feel guilty, either advertently or inadvertently?

_____

_____

71. What are the most effective resolutions to the prior two questions?

_____

_____

72. To what degree is your guilt self-imposed (I don't deserve this)? How can you overcome this internal reaction?

_____

_____

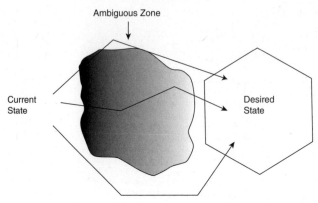

Figure 9.9 The Ambiguous Zone

73. What do you most have to let go of in order to reach out?

_____

_____

74. What baggage are you carrying that must be discarded?

_____

_____

75. What can you do daily to build the self-esteem muscle?

_____

_____

76. Are you in an ambiguous zone (Figure 9.9)? If so, how will you get through it?

_____

_____

77. If you were to start a journal, what entry would you make about the day preceding this one?

_____

_____

8. Sustaining the Journey

Building on strengths for constant growth

78. How would you characterize your current degree of generosity?

_____

_____

79. To what degree are you intellectually empathetic with others (identifying with their circumstances)?

_____

_____

80. To what degree are you emotionally empathetic with others (feeling what they feel)?

_____

_____

81. How well are you combining your passions and talents with your business synergistically?

_____

_____

82. When others tell you something can't be done or that they've failed trying, what is your usual response: forget about it, question the reasons, try to do what they did better, try to do it another way entirely?

_____

_____

83. How many brand-new activities or areas have you explored over the past year?

_____

_____

84. Choose two areas brand-new to you that you'd like to explore. How will you go about it?

_____

_____

85. How would you characterize your degree of autonomy?

_____

_____

86. Where can you apply the risk components of probability and seriousness in the near future for a significant decision?

_____

_____

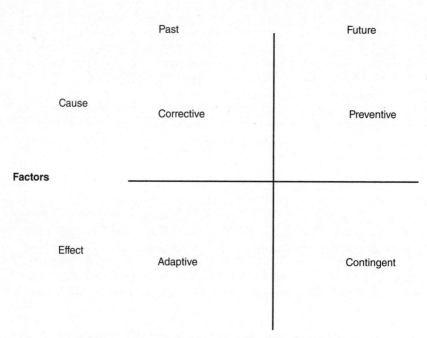

Figure 9.10   The Types of Actions Available

87. In which of the areas shown in Figure 9.10 do you spend most of your time? How can you become more flexible in using them all?

   _____

   _____

88. What types of relationships are you best at building? Should you be exploring other types?

   _____

   _____

89. What are you giving (offering) in order to receive?

   _____

   _____

90. How well do you develop trust quickly and sustain it?

   _____

   _____

91. Do you usually have a win/win attitude? How is it manifested?

_____

_____

92. Are you able to change relationships as some become inappropriate and new ones become more appropriate?

_____

_____

93. What's the contribution to your legacy you provided yesterday?

_____

_____

94. Do you ask yourself when considering a major decision, "What if everyone knew about this?" What impact does that have on your process?

_____

_____

95. Do you ask yourself when considering a major decision, "What if everyone did this?" What impact does that have on your process?

_____

_____

96. Do you ask yourself, "Is this a model I want to establish for my family and friends?" What impact does that have on your process?

_____

_____

97. What contribution to your legacy would you like to make tomorrow?

_____

_____

98. How would you like people to remember you in a unique way, so that everyone knew the description represents your life?

_____

_____

99. What is your greatest personal lesson from this book?

_____

_____

100. What is the most important question you now have about your journey that we haven't addressed, and how will you find the answer?

_____

_____

Feel free to write to Alan Weiss (alan@summitconsulting.com) _for complimentary tools and aids in creating and sustaining your journey._

For additional resources from Marshall Goldsmith, please visit www .marshallgoldsmith.com _or write to him at_ marshall@marshallgold smith.com.

Index